Back in the Days of Jesus:
Gospel Homilies
for Children

Matthew

©1996 by Living the Good News, Inc.

Living the Good News, Inc.
a division of The Morehouse Group
Editorial Offices
600 Grant Street, Suite 400
Denver, CO 80203

James R. Creasey, Publisher

Homilies by Dina Gluckstern and Dirk deVries

Editorial Staff: Joanne Youngquist, Kathleen Mulhern, Dirk deVries, Liz Riggleman,
   Dina Gluckstern, Kathy Coffey
Prepress/Production Staff: Sue MacStravic, Noel Taylor, Val Price, Meg Sandoval Phillips
Cover Design and Layout: Val Price, Sue MacStravic
Illustrations: Marcy Ramsey, Anne Kosel, Ansgar Holmberg, Betsy Johnson, Victoria Bergesen

Printed in the United States of America.

The scripture quotations used herein are from the Today's English Version, ©1992, American Bible Society. Used by permission.

ISBN 0-8192-8010-0 (Volume 1)
ISBN 1-889108-04-9 (4 Volume Set)

Table of Contents

Introduction

You invite them forward with a mixture of both joy and apprehension, these children of assorted sizes and ages. Adults shift to allow the escape from cramped pews and closely packed chairs. Small forms drop out into the aisles, then bob forward toward the front of the church, some holding hands, some looking back questioningly at parents. Many grin; others share your apprehension. They surround you, watching you closely, waiting for your smile, your touch, your greeting. You know you take a risk each time you welcome this unpredictable group forward, but you also know, as you settle together at the front of the church, that the next few minutes will be among the most rewarding of your week.

Each parish calls it something different: a children's message, perhaps, or a children's sermon or children's talk. Here we refer to it as a children's homily, a short presentation, based on the day's gospel reading, that invites the children to enter into and experience the story of our faith. Each homily respects the children's own spiritual vitality, urging them to share their experience of God, themselves and each other in an environment of love and safety.

Why offer children their own homily?

Offering a children's homily says to the children: "This is a special time just for you, because *church is for you, too.* Here, in church, you are welcomed, delighted in, treasured, held in our arms as you are held in God's arms." A children's homily extends in a concrete way the embrace of our loving God to include these, God's most vulnerable children. "You are this important to us," is the message, as the children file forward to gather for their homily.

But a children's homily offers the children more than the important affirmation that church is their place, too. A well-prepared children's homily couches the basics of Christian experience in terms the children understand and own. It invites children to experience the truths of scripture from the inside out: Children don't learn *about* Jesus calming the storm, they imagine themselves, frightened and rain-soaked, clinging to the sides of the rocking boat, yearning for safety, holding their breath for the moment when Jesus says "Peace, be still," feeling the relief that Jesus brings to the storms they experience in day-to-day life.

Children don't learn about the comfort of Jesus' hug, they exchange Jesus' hugs with each other, then take those hugs out into the congregation. You get the idea.

And the benefits of a children's homily go farther than the children themselves. If you regularly present children's homilies, you already know how often adults approach you after the service and say, "That was great. I got more out of your children's homily than the regular homily." A children's homily—perhaps *because* it presents its point so simply and clearly, with the added framework of childlike wonder and innocence—can profoundly impress and move. Never underestimate the power of a child's fresh perspective or sudden and unexpected insight.

Many of the adults watching from the pews don't have children, or have little regular contact with small children. The children's homily helps balance their lives with the wonder and delight the children take in these encounters with God and scripture.

In addition, when you present the children's homilies, you model for families, friends and relatives ways to engage the children they love in the journey of faith. Story-telling, movement, songs, games and the use of props and illustrations—all of these explore faith in simple ways that others can use as well. After a month or two of watching children's homilies, people begin to catch on, even unconsciously adopting the methods demonstrated in your children's homilies.

Who are these homilies for?

Back in the Days of Jesus: Gospel Homilies for Children from the Gospel of Matthew contains forty-six homilies, written for children from the age of four or five through eleven or twelve. Admittedly, this is a broad age range, and you may find some homilies seem more appropriate for the younger children than the older. We have attempted to provide something for all ages in each homily, including occasionally offering options within the homilies themselves. Keep in mind that a children's homily is not an instructional activity, and that age matters less when sharing in ritual and worship. In fact, a variety of responses can enrich the experience for all participants. You may want to invite older children to help younger children with certain tasks and responses. The older children will benefit from the sense of awe and wonder—the raw spirituality—of the younger children.

These homilies will work for both small and large groups, from less than half a dozen to as many as thirty or more. When appropriate, we suggest ways to change the homily for very small or very large groups; for example, in a large group, you may not be able to invite every child to offer a response to every question; do your best to let different children answer each question. In a small group, you may be able to reproduce a simple prop for each child to take home. For the most part, the size of the group will not matter, but if it does, you should be able to adapt each homily for the number of children you anticipate coming forward.

If you regularly have a larger group (more than twelve), consider recruiting another adult or teenage helper for each additional six or so children. This is particularly helpful when the homily includes more complex activities, or if another leader can provide a calming influence for restless children.

How do I prepare?

Each homily in this book includes:
- a scripture reference
- a quote from the reading
- a brief summary of both the reading and the homily
- a materials list
- directions for the homily
- a suggestion for closing prayer

We encourage you to begin your preparation by reading the scripture on which the homily is based. You might consider reading the story in two Bible versions, including *Today's English Version,* used in the preparation of these homilies. Think about the passage. You might ask yourself:
- What does this reading say to me?
- What truth about God, about others or about myself do I learn from this reading?

Then extend your question to include the children you anticipate will join you for the homily:
- What would I like the children to hear in this story?
- What does this reading say to them about the love and care of God?

After your own consideration of the reading, read through the summary of the reading and the homily, check the materials list and read once through the homily itself.

Most homilies in this book offer both an age-appropriate retelling of the gospel story and at least one activity to help the children enter into the meaning of the story (occasionally both story and activity are blended into one overall activity). Time limitations or personal preference may require that you use one or the other rather than both. Feel free to do so. The stories can stand alone; if you wish, a question or two taken from the activity may be enough to help you draw a story-only homily to a conclusion. Likewise, you may not wish to retell the gospel story if it has just been read from the Bible or lectionary; in this case, simply follow the regular reading of scripture with the homily activity.

Once you decide how much of the homily you wish to present, gather your materials and practice telling the story. We encourage you to memorize the story, though you may certainly use your own words if you wish. Tell the story to yourself, a friend or a family member once or twice. Inexperienced at storytelling? Familiarize yourself with the two cardinal rules of storytelling—make eye contact with your listeners and make sure they can hear you!

At the conclusion of each homily we offer a prayer. Again, add to or adapt each prayer as you wish.

Some basic principles to keep in mind:
- *The younger the children, the*

shorter the homily. One guideline suggests that children will sit still and listen one minute for each year of their age; for example, the average five-year-old will be there, attending to you, for five minutes, an eight-year-old for eight minutes. Keep that in mind at points in the homily when you are doing the talking, for example, during a non-participatory story. That's why these homilies incorporate lots of movement and interaction.

- *There are more people involved than you and the children.* The parishioners listen and participate along with the children. Face the parishioners as you sit down to present the homily. Speak loudly, slowly and clearly. Repeat answers given by children if the children speak too softly for the parishioners to hear. If you use a poster or another prop, make it big enough—and hold it up high enough—for the parishioners to see, too. If children participate in actions (other than in a circle or semi-circle facing inward), face them toward the parishioners. While you and the children are not performing for the parishioners, you do invite them to worship with you. Keep that in mind.

- *Respect what children say.* You don't need to correct the children, you need only allow them to experience the story for themselves, to find their own meaning and, if they wish, to articulate that meaning. God reveals God's self to children, as to adults, in the right ways at

the right times. Trust God to do this in your children's homilies.

In the homily, affirm all children for their responses; a simple thank-you accomplishes this beautifully. You can also say, "Jared, you believe..." or "Deanna, you feel like...," reflecting back to children what they have shared. Acknowledge each child's right to believe and feel whatever he or she believes and feels without editorializing. At times you may be hoping the children suggest a specific idea; if they do not, simply suggest the idea yourself. Your ideas matter too, and the children want to hear them.

- *Expect the unexpected.* In these homilies you invite open responses from creative, uninhibited children. You cannot control what they say or do (nor would you want to). If they perceive you as a caring friend, they will want to tell you about their pets, toys, eating habits and other topics that you may prefer not to discuss when you are leading in front of your parishioners. This will happen. Expect it, flow with it and enjoy it. Welcome even off-the-wall comments with grace and good humor, but be cautious not to laugh at the children, even when the parishioners do. A child can easily feel hurt if a serious comment shared in trust is met with laughter. Show your respect for the children by responding appreciatively to whatever they say.

Deal with the unexpected comment by acknowledging the

child and redirecting attention back to the story or activity. If a child continues, you can thank him or her for the desire to share and explain that now you would like to focus on the activity or story at hand. Ask the child, "May I listen to your story later, after church?" Be sure to follow through with the child later. You might also put your finger to your lips and say, "This is our quiet time, our time to listen to the story. Can you do that for us?"

It always helps to remember: The clearest message to the children does not come through the content of your homily, but through the loving relationship you offer them when you gather together.

On Sunday morning, make sure to bring your collected materials and this book. Take a few minutes for a final review. Place any needed materials unobtrusively near the area where you will gather the children.

We recommend that you gather at the front of the church. Children can sit in a semicircle around you on the floor. If the floor is not carpeted, consider purchasing a large square carpet remnant to make sitting more comfortable. Many churches have several low steps at the front of the church; you could sit on one of these or on a low stool. You could, of course, also sit with the children on the floor.

Once you and the children settle in, begin the homily. Look with love and respect at each young face before you. You are in for a treat: these children have invited you into a most sacred circle. Consider yourself honored...and see what God will do.

Dirk deVries

One final note: Looking for a reading not covered in this volume? That reading may have a parallel in one or more of the other gospels— Mark, Luke or John. Look in the other volumes of *Back in the Days of Jesus: Gospel Homilies for Children* and you may find the homily you seek.

■ ■ ■ ■ ■

Matthew 1:18-25

"Joseph, descendant of David, do not be afraid to take Mary to be your wife. She will have a son, and you will call him Jesus —because he will save his people from their sins." (Matthew 1:20b-21, *Today's English Version***)**

Summary

In this reading from the Gospel of Matthew, Joseph decides to divorce the pregnant Mary—until an angel comes, in a dream, to assure him that Mary bears God's promised Messiah. In today's homily, children hear and pantomime today's gospel story, then discuss the angel's message to Joseph: "Do not be afraid!"

Materials

Bible
3 blankets or sleeping bags
3 child-sized bath robes

Homily

Invite the children to come forward for today's homily.

Recruit nine of the children (or six or three in smaller groups) to pantomime today's story as you tell it. Divide these nine children into groups of three. Ask *one* child in *each* group to play the part of Mary, one the part of Joseph and one the part of the angel. (You'll

have three complete sets of actors.) Give each *Joseph* a blanket or sleeping bag and each *angel* a robe. Invite the groups of three to silently act out the story as you tell it to the remaining children.

Ask the remaining children to sit in a semicircle around you. Hold the Bible open to the Gospel of Matthew as you tell today's story:

Joseph wants to ask Mary a very important question. Joseph feels nervous. What if Mary says no?

Joseph takes a big gulp. "Will you marry me?" he asks Mary.

"Yes," says Mary. "I will marry you." Joseph sighs in relief. He feels very happy.

One day Mary finds out that she is going to have a baby, a very special baby named Jesus.

Mary says to Joseph, "Joseph, I'm going to have a baby."

"A baby!" Joseph cries. "But we aren't even married yet! You cannot have a baby!"

"Yes, I can," said Mary. "I can have God's special baby, Jesus."

"I do not believe you. I will not marry you," says angry Joseph.

That night, angry Joseph falls fast asleep. He dreams about Mary. An angel comes into his dream with a message from God.

"Joseph," the angel whispers. "Do not be afraid. Do not be afraid to marry Mary. You can believe her. God promises you that she will have a baby. The baby will be God's Son, Jesus. Do not be afraid, Joseph."

Joseph wakes up. "Thank you, God," he says. "Thank you for your promise! Now I can marry Mary. Now I can take care of your Son Jesus."

Thank the actors, ask them to be seated, and, if you wish, follow the story with a brief discussion:
- What did the angel whisper to Joseph? *("Do not be afraid.")*
- When are we sometimes afraid?
- Let's say the angel's message to each other!

Invite children to say in unison with you several times:
- Do not be afraid! Do not be afraid!

Prayer

- Thank you, God, that you said to angry, frightened Joseph, "Don't be afraid!" We are glad you are always with us, so we don't have to fear either. *Amen.*

Thank the children for joining you and invite them to return to their seats.

■ ■ ■ ■ ■

Matthew 2:1-12

**"Where is the baby born to be the king
of the Jews? We saw his star when
it came up in the east, and we have
come to worship him."** (Matthew 2:2,
Today's English Version)

Summary

In this reading from the Gospel of
Matthew, searchers from the East
come to worship the baby Jesus. In
today's homily, children hear the
story of the visit of the magi and
share what gifts they would like to
give the baby Jesus.

Materials

Bible
large star cut from cardboard and
    covered with aluminum foil,
    hung as high as possible on the
    wall to one side of your parish
    worship space
manger or cradle placed beneath
    the star
baby doll wrapped in simple cloth
    and placed in manger

Homily

Invite the children to come forward for today's homily. Gather to
the side opposite where you have
hung the star.

Ask the children to be seated in a
semicircle around you. Hold the
Bible open to the Gospel of
Matthew as you tell today's story:

Who can tell me the name of
the town where Jesus was
born? *(Pause for children's
answers.)* That's right,
Bethlehem!

Jesus' mother wrapped him up
all warm and snug. She wanted
to lay him in a cradle, but she
didn't have one. Where did
Jesus' mother put him that first
night? *(Pause for children's answers.)* That's right, in a
manger!

Well, while Jesus was sleeping,
safe and warm in that manger,
other people, a long way away,
in a country far to the East,
were looking up into the night
sky, wondering about all God's
many stars.

Then they saw a special star...a star that may have looked like that star right over there. *(Direct children's attention to the star hung on the opposite wall.)* Can we all see the star? *(Pause for children's answers.)*

They studied that special star very carefully. They opened their big star books and consulted their ancient star charts. They talked to each other in excited whispers: "Something important has happened. The special star tells us so. A king has been born. A very special baby. This baby will grow up to bring joy and peace and light to all the world."

The more they talked, the more excited they became. "Let's go see this baby. Let's follow this star!"

So they packed up their books and charts and started traveling, following the special star, all the way to Bethlehem, just to visit the baby Jesus.

Shall we follow the star, too? *(Invite children to move with you to the other side of the church. Sit together in front of the manger or cradle)*

Do you know what the visitors from the East did when they finally found Jesus? *(Pause for children's answers.)* That's right, they gave him precious gifts—gold, frankincense and myrrh. And they knelt down and they worshiped Jesus, the special baby.

Set aside the Bible and ask:
■ If we could each give the baby Jesus just *one* gift this morning, what would it be?

Invite all children who wish to share an opportunity to do so.

Prayer
■ Jesus, accept the gifts we bring you. *Amen.*

Thank the children for joining you and invite them to return to their seats.

Matthew 2: 13-15, 19-23

An angel of the Lord appeared in a dream to Joseph and said, "Herod will be looking for the child in order to kill him. So get up, take the child and his mother and escape to Egypt, and stay there until I tell you to leave." (Matthew 2:13, *Today's English Version*)

Summary

In this reading from the Gospel of Matthew, Joseph, Mary and Jesus escape Herod's wrath by fleeing to Egypt. In today's homily, children hear this gospel story and discuss what it means to be part of a family.

Material

Bible
poster on which you have written:
   A family is...
felt marker

Homily

Invite the children to come forward for today's homily. Ask them to be seated in a semicircle around you. Hold the Bible open to the Gospel of Matthew as you tell today's story:

After Jesus was born, after the shepherds had gone back to their sheep, Joseph lay down to sleep. An angel came to Joseph as he dreamed.

"Joseph," said the angel, "you must take the child Jesus and his mother Mary and run away to Egypt. King Herod wants to kill this child."

Joseph awoke. He shook Mary awake. "Hurry!" he said, "We must leave at once! King Herod wants to kill Jesus!"

Mary got up. Joseph gathered the child in his arms. They ran into the night, under the stars, out of the town of Bethlehem.

Joseph and Mary walked for many days. The nights were cold, the desert days were hot, and the way to Egypt was long.

And the days in Egypt were long, too. Joseph and Mary wanted to go home, back to

the land and the people they knew. "But we can't," said Mary. "Not while King Herod is alive to kill Jesus."

One night in Egypt, as Joseph slept, he dreamed again. Again an angel came. "King Herod is dead," said the angel. "Go back to your home."

The next day Joseph told Mary about his dream. "Thank God," said Mary. "Now we can go back home."

Jesus, Mary and Joseph began the long journey back. They met travelers on the road. And one traveler had scary news. "Archelaus, the son of Herod, is the new King," said this traveler.

"Archelaus!" whispered Mary to Joseph. "Surely he is as cruel as King Herod ever was!"

Joseph's heart was sad when he lay down to sleep that night. But once more, an angel appeared in Joseph's dream. "Do not go back to Bethlehem in Judea," said the angel. "Go instead to the town of Nazareth in Galilee. Archelaus will not find Jesus there."

Joseph woke up glad. "Again God has sent an angel to guide us. God has kept this family safe once more."

Show children the poster on which you have written, "A family is..." Read these words aloud and ask:
■ How could we finish this sentence?

Encourage many answers; write all answers on the poster. *Examples*:
■ A family is...
  — big
  — nice
  — a mother and father and kids
  — people together

If necessary, you can stimulate more answers by changing the question slightly:
■ What makes a family?
■ Pretend a Martian from outer space has landed. The Martian comes to you and says, "I don't understand this word *family*. What is a family?" How would you answer?

Continue recording all answers until the children have given at least a dozen ways to finish the sentence. Then say:
■ God made Joseph, Mary and Jesus into a family. God makes us a family, too. Let's remind each other that we belong to God's family.

Turn to the child on your left and say:
■ "*(Child's name)*, you belong to God's family."

Help the children pass this affirmation around the semicircle.

Prayer
■ Thank you, God, for the family of Jesus, Mary and Joseph. Thank you, God, for the family of each person here. *Amen.*

Thank the children for joining you and invite them to return to their seats.

Matthew 3:1-12

"Turn away from your sins," he said, "because the Kingdom of heaven is near!" (Matthew 3:2, *Today's English Version*)

Summary

In this reading from the Gospel of Matthew, John the Baptist prepares God's people for the coming Messiah: Jesus. In today's homily, children hear the story of John's preaching and sing a simple song about preparing for Jesus' coming.

Materials

Bible
optional:
accompanist for song "Prepare the Way," printed below

Homily

Invite the children to come forward for today's homily. Ask the children to sit in a semicircle around you.

Hold the Bible open to the Gospel of Matthew as you tell today's story:

Who is this odd man? He lives all alone out in the desert. Do *we* live all alone out in the desert?

And he dresses in clothes made of camel's hair! Do *we* wear clothes made out of camel's hair?

And he eats grasshoppers with honey. Do *we* eat grasshoppers with honey?

His name is John, and what's that he's saying? "Someone's coming!" John tells the people. "Someone's coming who brings light wherever it's dark."

Wherever it's dark. Hmm. Can *we* think of dark places that need light? *(Pause for children's responses.)*

"Someone's coming!" John tells the people. "Someone's coming who brings peace wherever there's hurt."

Wherever there's hurt. Hmm. Can *we* think of hurting people who need peace? *(Pause for children's responses.)*

"Someone's coming!" John tells the people. "Someone's coming who brings good news to God's people."

Good news. Hmm. Can *we* think of people who could use some good news? *(Pause for children's responses.)*

"*Who's* coming?" ask the people. "*Who* brings light and peace and good news?"

"Jesus!" says John. "Jesus is coming! Get ready for Jesus."

Teach the children the song "Prepare the Way," printed below. If you're not comfortable leading the children in singing, chant the words in rhythm.

Prayer

■ Come, Lord Jesus, to all of us who get ready for you here, as John the Baptist helped people get ready for you so long ago. *Amen.*

Invite the children *and the parishioners* to once again sing the song (or chant the words) as the children return to their seats.

PREPARE THE WAY

Words and music by Pamela L. Hughes

Pre-pare, pre-pare, pre-pare the way for Je-sus in your heart. Pre-pare, pre-pare, pre-pare the way. Come on, it's time to start! We'll skip a - long and sing our song as we pre - pare the way for Je - sus' birth right here on earth, that bless-ed Christ-mas day!

■ ■ ■ ■ ■

Matthew 3:13-17

As soon as Jesus was baptized, he came up out of the water. Then heaven opened to him, and he saw the Spirit of God coming down like a dove and lighting on him. (Matthew 3:16, *Today's English Version***)**

Summary

In this reading from the Gospel of Matthew, John baptizes Jesus in the Jordan River, and God identifies Jesus as God's "own dear Son." In today's homily, children hear this story and explore the meaning of baptism.

Materials

Bible
washable doll
bowl of water
baptismal shell or ordinary shell
   for scooping water

Homily

Invite the children to come forward for today's homily. Ask the children to sit in a semicircle around you.

Encourage children to recall baptisms they have seen in church. Adapt questions to fit your own parish practices; for example:
■ Have you seen the priest pour water on babies during church? What happened?
■ When do we use water in

church? What happens in the water?

Use the doll and basin to act out the rite of baptism. You might pray, "God, make this child your child," as you use a shell or the parish baptismal shell to dip water over the doll's head. Use a few words and gestures most likely to recall the act of baptism for the children.

Close by saying:
■ In our church, we baptize with water in a font. *(Modify to fit your parish's practice.)*
■ Sometimes people use water in a river to baptize, too.
■ Someone comes to a river to be baptized in today's story. Listen and find out who!

Hold the Bible open to the Gospel of Matthew as you tell today's story:

John comes to the water of the river Jordan. "Come," he calls to the people. "Come to the water."

The people come, from markets and meadows. The people

19

come, from streets and store-houses. The people come to the water of the river Jordan.

"Come to the water," John says to the people. "Come and be baptized."

The people come to John. John plunges them into and out of the water. "Now you are baptized," John says.

Jesus comes to the water. He calls to John, "Baptize me."

John says, "No, Jesus, you should baptize me!"

But Jesus says, "John, this is what God wants."

So Jesus wades into the water. John plunges Jesus into and out of the water.

As Jesus comes up out of the water he sees the heavens open up. The Spirit of God comes down like a graceful, white bird to be with Jesus.

A voice from the clouds says, "Jesus is my own dear Child. I am pleased with him."

Prayer

■ Thank you, God, for calling Jesus your Child. Thank you for calling us your children, too. *Amen.*

Thank the children for joining you and invite them to return to their seats.

■ ■ ■ ■ ■

Matthew 4:1-11

Jesus answered, "The scripture says, 'Human beings cannot live on bread alone, but need every word that God speaks.'" (Matthew 4:4, *Today's English Version*)

Summary

In this reading from the Gospel of Matthew, the devil tempts Jesus to give up his trust in God. In today's homily, children hear this story and experiment with trusting you, the homilist.

Materials

Bible
bag of individual, small treats for the children, for example, dimes or quarters, miniature candy bars, suckers, bookmarks, etc., 1 per child

Homily

Invite the children to come forward for today's homily. Ask the children to sit in a semicircle around you.

Say to the children:
■ I have a special treat for each of you.
■ I'll give you your treat, but I want you to just hold it in your hand for now, okay?

Distribute the treat. Let children respond. You could ask:

■ What will you do with your treat?
■ Is this a treat you like a lot? a little?

After a minute or two of discussion, say:
■ Now I'd like you to give me your treat back. You don't *have* to give them to me, but I'd like you to.
■ I promise I'll give them back to you again after I tell today's story.
■ Do you trust me?

Collect as many treats as children will return to you. Allow children who wish to keep their treats to do so. Discuss:
■ What does it mean to trust someone?
■ Let's see whom Jesus trusts in today's story.

Jesus walked through the desert. It was very hot. (*Invite children to pretend they are hot.*)

And Jesus was very tired. (*Invite children to pretend they are very tired.*)

And Jesus hadn't eaten for a long, long time, so he was very

hungry. *(Invite children to pretend they are very hungry.)*

The devil came to Jesus. "Mmm, I bet some nice, warm, fresh bread would taste good right now, wouldn't it, Jesus?"

It would, Jesus knew.

"If you're really God's Son," said the devil, "why don't you just turn some of these stones into bread and eat them?"

Jesus thought about it. He could do that, and then he wouldn't be hungry. But he decided no, he'd rather trust in God to take of his hunger. Jesus answered the devil, "I need more than bread to live; I need to listen to God."

The devil came to Jesus again. Together they stood way up on top of the temple. The devil said, "Jump; go ahead. If you're really God's Son, angels will take care of you. You won't get hurt."

Jesus thought about it. He could do that, and it might be kind of fun. But he decided no, he'd rather trust in God to take care of him. Jesus answered the devil, "It's not good to test God; I'll just trust God instead."

The devil came to Jesus a third time. They stood on a high mountain. "Look at all you can see," said the devil. "If you trust in me instead of God, I'll let you rule all you can see—I'll let you rule the whole world."

Jesus thought about it. Ruling the world might be awesome— he'd be in charge of everyone! But he decided no, he'd rather let God rule the world, and he would trust God to do it right. Jesus answered the devil, "Go away. I'll worship God only, not you. I'll trust in God alone."

And the devil left.

If you wish, discuss with children:
■ When do we trust God?
■ How do we show God our trust in God?

Return children's treats to them.

Prayer

■ God, help us to trust you. Help us to trust in your love and strength. *Amen.*

Thank the children for joining you and invite them to return to their seats.

22

Matthew 4:12-23

Jesus said to them, "Come with me, and I will teach you to catch people. At once they left their nets and went with him." (Matthew 4:19-20, *Today's English Version*)

Summary

In today's reading from the Gospel of Matthew, Jesus invites four fishermen to become his first disciples, "fishers of people." In today's homily, children participate in the telling of the story, then reach out to "catch" the entire parish.

Materials

Bible
a fishing net, a mesh bag, a piece of net cloth or a pillowcase

Homily

Invite the children to come forward for today's homily. Ask them to be seated in a semicircle around you.

Ask the children, "How can we catch fish?" The answer will probably be, "with a fishing pole." Show the children your net and explain how it works. Let each child have a chance to hold it. Tell the children that the fishers in today's story use nets to fish.

Hold the Bible open to the Gospel of Matthew as you tell today's story:

Jesus says, "It's time for me to tell everyone about God's love." So Jesus goes walking. *(Pretend to walk in place.)*

"I need friends to help me," says Jesus. "I need friends to follow me."*(Shade eyes with hand.)*

He walks along the shore of a lake. *(Walk in place.)*

Then Jesus sees Andrew and Simon fishing. *(Shade eyes with hand.)*

Jesus says, "Come with me, Andrew and Simon. *(Motion for two children to come to you.)*

"I'll teach you to catch people for God." *(Spread the "net.")*

They all walk on along the lake. *(Walk in place with two children.)*

Jesus sees James and John fishing. *(Shade eyes with hand.)*

Jesus says, "Come with me, James and John. *(Motion for two more children to come to you.)*

"I'll teach you to catch people for God."

(Spread "net.")

They all walk on together. *(Walk in place with four children.)*

"No more catching fish," says Jesus. *(Lay net aside.)*

"Now I'll teach you to catch people for God." *(Walk with four children to all other children. Help children take any child still sitting by the hand, until all the children are walking together.)*

Gather children around you and say:
- God wants *all* people to be caught for God.
- Shall we catch all *these* people for God? *(Indicate to children the parishioners.)*

After children have responded, spread out, hand-in-hand with the children, to encompass as many parishioners as possible. Say the prayer as you stand this way with the children.

Prayer

- Dear Jesus, thanks for calling each one of us to come and follow you. *Amen.*

Thank the children for joining you and invite them to return to their seats.

Matthew 5:1-12

"Happy are those who know they are spiritually poor; the Kingdom of heaven belongs to them! Happy are those who are humble; they will receive what God has promised!" (Matthew 5:3, 5, *Today's English Version*)

Summary

Today's reading from the Gospel of Matthew presents the Beatitudes. These verses turn our typical way of thinking upside down, telling us, "Happy are those who mourn" and "Happy are those who are persecuted." Such paradoxes are difficult for young children to grasp. Children can, however, begin to understand that Jesus and God act in surprising ways. In today's homily, children first surprise each other with ever-changing clap-and-slap rhythms, then hear today's story.

Materials

Bible

Homily

Invite the children to come forward for today's homily. Ask them to be seated in a semicircle around you.

Begin a simple clap-and-slap pattern; for example, clap your hands together once, then slap your lap once. When all the children have joined in, call out, "Surprise!" and change the rhythm; for example, clap your hands together three times in front of you, then once over your head.

Ask the child to your left to continue the game with another surprise. Continue around the circle until several children have had the chance to call out "Surprise!" and lead the rhythm.

Say:
■ Listen for the surprises in today's story.

Hold the Bible open to the Gospel of Matthew as you tell today's story:

"I don't think I'm an important person," says a girl. "Presidents, teachers, parents—those are the important people."

25

"Surprise!" says Jesus. "You are just as important to me as any grown-up."

"Teachers and priests know a lot about God," says a boy. "I don't think I know very much."

"Surprise!" says Jesus. "All of God's heaven belongs to you."

"If I were a real Christian, I wouldn't get angry or hurt people," says one girl. "I don't think God is very happy with me."

"Surprise!" says Jesus. "God loves you, no matter what you've done. God will take away every sad feeling."

"I wish I could see God!" says one boy. "I wish I could really know God."

"Surprise!" says Jesus. "You already know God!

Prayer

Invite children to thank God for good surprises in their lives.

Close by praying:
■ Thank you, God, for all good surprises. *Amen.*

Thank the children for joining you and invite them to return to their seats.

26

Matthew 5:13-20

You are like salt for the whole human race. You are like light for the whole world. (Matthew 5:13a, 14a, *Today s English Version*)

Summary

In today's reading from the Gospel of Matthew, Jesus tells us that we are both salt and light for the world. In today's homily, children experiment with salt and light, hear today's story and learn a simple song about God's light.

Materials

Bible
salty foods, such as potato chips or
   pretzels
small stoneware jar with salt
votive candle hidden under a bowl
matches

Homily

Invite the children to come forward for today's homily. Ask them to be seated in a semicircle around you.

Distribute a pretzel or potato chip to each child. Before you eat these snacks, discuss:
■ What is salt?
■ What foods do we like that are salty?
■ Can you see the salt on your pretzel (or potato chip)?
■ Eat your pretzel (potato chip) and tell us if you taste the salt.

■ Let's here what Jesus says about salt in today's story.

Hold the Bible open to the Gospel of Matthew as you tell today's story:

One day Jesus and his friends sat on a hill as he told them stories. Here are two such stories:

In a house there was a room. In the room there was a corner. In the corner there was a jar. In the jar there was salt. *(Hold up the jar of salt.)* Salt to make the food taste good! Salt to make the cucumbers into pickles! Salt to keep the meat fresh!

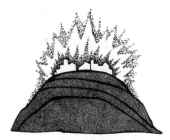

"Look at these greens I found at the market," called the man of the house to the woman of the house. "Let's salt them away!"

"We'll feast on them for months," said the woman happily. She fetched the stone jar filled with

27

salt. She licked her finger, stuck it in the jar and took a taste. *(Lick your finger, stick it in the jar, and taste.)* She stopped smiling.

"No taste! This salt has no taste at all!" said the woman. "There's nothing to do with it except throw it out."

In another house there was another room. In this room there was a bowl. And under this bowl something was hidden. *(Show bowl.)*

"Why is it so dark in here?" said a woman, as she walked into the room. She looked around the room for the lamp. *(Peer around you as if in darkness.)*

"We need some light," said a man, as he walked into the room. He ran his hands along the walls, trying to find the lamp. *(Feel around you as if in darkness.)*

"It's night now," said a girl, as she walked into the room. "Let's light the lamp." And she began to peer into each corner.

She found nothing in the first corner. Nothing in the second corner. But in the third corner she bumped into the bowl. The bowl tipped over— and there was the lamp. *(Bump into bowl and remove it from the candle.)*

"What a silly place to put a lamp," the girl laughed. And she set it on a lamp stand where it gave light to the whole house. *(Light the lamp.)*

Sing these words to the tune of "Praise God From Whom All Blessings Flow"; if you don't know this tune, simply chant the words in rhythm:

> We see God's light shine in our hearts.
> We see God's light shine in our friends.
> We see God's light shine in God's world.
> We see God's light shine without end.

Prayer

■ Dear God, thanks for making us like salt and light for our families and friends. *Amen.*

■ ■ ■ ■ ■

Matthew 5:21-24

**"So if you are about to offer your gift
to God at the altar and there you
remember that your brother has
something against you, leave your gift
there in front of the altar, go at once
and make peace with your brother,
and then come back and offer your
gift to God." (Matthew 5:23-24,**
*Today's English Version***)**

Summary

In this reading from the Gospel of
Matthew, Jesus admonishes his disciples to make peace with one another when they are angry. In today's homily, children first hear and
discuss the gospel story, then learn
and sing a simple song about making peace when they are angry.

Materials

Bible

Homily

Invite the children to come forward for today's homily. Ask them
to be seated in a semicircle around
you.

Hold the Bible open to the Gospel
of Matthew as you tell today's
story:

**"You good-for-nothing!" yelled
Micah to his brother, Daniel.**

**Micah stomped out of Daniel's
house. "I'm never coming to
your house again!" Micah
yelled.**

**Micah was on his way to the
temple. He was taking bundles
of wheat to offer to God. But
he barely remembered the
grain in his arms as he fussed
and fumed all the way to the
temple.**

**Micah entered the gate to the
temple. He saw the priest helping people bring gifts to the
altar. Micah started to walk to
the priest, but he hadn't taken
three steps when he stopped.**

He couldn't stop thinking about Daniel. He remembered just how hurt Daniel had looked when Micah yelled out, "You good-for-nothing!"

Suddenly Micah left his gift right there in front of the altar and ran all the way back to Daniel's house.

"Daniel," he called, "I'm sorry I called you a name. I'll never do it again."

Daniel smiled. "I forgive you," he said.

Now Micah smiled, too, as he walked with a glad heart back to the temple. And there, at last, he brought his gift to the altar.

If you wish, discuss with the children:
■ When have we gotten angry with our moms or dads? our brothers or sisters? our friends?
■ What are some not-so-good ways we've handled our anger?
■ What are some really good ways we've handled our anger?

Invite children to sing "Sometimes We're Mad and We're Angry." The tune is "The Bear Went Over the Mountain" and the words are:

Sometimes we're mad and we're angry.
Sometimes we're mad and we're angry.
Sometimes we're mad and we're angry.
God says, "Here's what to do."

Oh, go make peace with your neighbor.
Oh, go make peace with your neighbor.
Oh, go make peace with your neighbor.
God says, "That's what to do."

Go tell your friend why you're angry.
Go tell your friend why you're angry.
Go tell your friend why you're angry.
God says, "That's what to do."

Invite the children to make up vigorous movements to illustrate each verse; for example, children could jump up and shake their fists as they sing "Sometimes we're mad and we're angry."

Prayer

Turn to a child standing next to you and say:
■ The peace of the Lord be with you. (Or "Peace be with you," or simply "Peace.")

Invite that child to turn to the next child and repeat this blessing of peace. Continue until this blessing has gone all the way around the circle. Then invite the children to say it in unison to the parishioners.

Close by praying:
■ God, thank you for peace between friends, peace between family members and peace in our world. Amen.

Thank the children for joining you and invite them to return to their seats.

■ ■ ■ ■ ■

Matthew 5:38-48

"You have heard that it was said, 'Love your friends, hate your enemies.' But now I tell you: love your enemies and pray for those who persecute you..." (Matthew 5:43-44, *Today's English Version*)

Summary

In this reading from the Gospel of Matthew, Jesus teaches love for enemies. In today's homily, children hear the story, then think of ways to show kindness to less-than-friendly people.

Materials

Bible
large stuffed animal, the less cute the better

Homily

Invite the children to come forward for today's homily. Ask them to sit in a semicircle around you.

Invite children to discuss:
■ Tell me about a time when someone was unkind to you or hurt you.
■ How do we feel when people are mean to us?
■ What do we do when people are mean to us?

Show the stuffed animal. Say:
■ Let's imagine that this animal is a mean animal, one who likes to

break our toys, call us names and tell bad stories about us. Let's call this mean ol' animal *Grrr*.
■ What would we like to say to ol' Grrr about being so mean?

Set Grrr aside as you say:
■ Let's see what Jesus has to say about people who are mean to us.

Hold the Bible open to the Gospel of Matthew as you tell today's story:

One day, Jesus sat with his friends and talked about what to do when someone is mean to you.

"I know what to do," said one friend. "If he's mean to me, I'm mean right back to him."

"Yes," said another friend. "If she hits me, I hit her back, only harder."

"If people call me names," said the first friend," I call them *worse* names."

31

"Wait," said Jesus. "I have a better way. If someone is mean to you, I want you to be nice to them. If someone hurts you, I want you to love them."

"What!?" said all of Jesus' friends at once. "You want us to *love* our enemies? Be *kind* to those who hurt us?" They looked at each other in dismay. That would be awfully hard.

Jesus said, "Do not take revenge on someone who wrongs you. You have heard people say to love your friends and hate your enemies. But now I tell you: love your enemies; pray for them; help them."

"God loves everyone, even the people who don't like you. God wants you to love everyone too."

Pick up Grrr and ask:
■ How could we show our love for Grrr, this mean ol' animal?

As children make suggestions, let them hold and express their love for Grrr.

Conclude the homily by saying:
■ I think all this love may make Grrr a much nicer animal. What do *you* think?

Prayer

■ Dear God, it's not always easy to love people who aren't nice to us. Help us to do this, for Jesus sake. *Amen.*

Thank the children for joining you and invite them to return to their seats.

■ ■ ■ ■ ■

Matthew 6:5-14

"But when you pray, go to your room, close the door, and pray to your Father, who is unseen. And your Father, who sees what you do in private, will reward you." (Matthew 6:6, *Today's English Version*)

Summary

In this reading from the Gospel of Matthew, Jesus teaches his disciples about prayer. In today's homily, the children witness those prayer behaviors Jesus discourages, then pray themselves as Jesus suggests in the gospel story.

Materials

Bible

Homily

Invite the children to come forward for today's homily. Ask the children to sit in a semicircle around you.

If you wish, begin the homily with a brief discussion:
■ What is prayer?
■ When do we pray?
■ How do we pray?
■ Jesus once taught his disciples about prayer, and that's the story I want to tell you today.

Hold the Bible open to the Gospel of Matthew as you tell today's story:

Jesus and his friends sat together on a hill. The sun shone brightly. Birds sailed high overhead, catching bugs.

"Teach us about prayer," said one disciple.

"First of all," Jesus said, "don't pray like this:" *(Stand up and offer the following prayer in a loud voice, with plenty of pompous, dramatic gesturing.)*

Ahem... *(clearing your throat to gather attention).* **God, thanks for making me such a wonderful person...much more wonderful than those people over there...or those people over there. Thanks for helping**

me be so very spiritual...and so very loving...and so very, very good.

(Sit down as you continue.) "No," said Jesus. "You don't need to pray so everyone hears and thinks you're great. You can pray anytime, including when you are all alone. God always hears you."

Jesus continued: "And don't pray like this, either:" *(Stand up again and offer the following prayer in a similar loud voice, with plenty of dramatic gesturing.)*

> Oh, magnificent Trinitarian Deity, splendid, astounding, wonder-working Divine Presence, above and beyond we mere mortals who struggle to survive the capricious vicissitudes of existence here in the midst of your ever-renewing creation...

(Sit down as you continue.) "No," said Jesus. "You don't need fancy words when you pray. God knows what you need before you even start. Just talk to God like you talk to a friend."

"Here's how you can pray," Jesus said. "When you pray, you can let God know that you love and honor God."

What could we say to God right now that let's God know how much we love and honor God? *(Welcome all responses from the children. If necessary, offer a prayer or two to get them started: We love you, God. We think you're great, God. Your birds and trees are beautiful, God.)*

Jesus said, "When you pray, you can ask God for the things you need."

What could we ask God for right now? *(Again welcome all responses from the children. If necessary, suggest some beginning prayers: God, give us the food we need each day. Dear God, help heal my friend who is sick with the flu.)*

Jesus said, "When you pray, you can thank God for God's good gifts to us."

What would we like to thank God for, right now? *(Welcome responses. If necessary, encourage children by praying: Dear God, thank you for our moms and dads. Thank you for my dog, Rex.)*

"That's how you can pray!" Jesus said.

Prayer

Close today's homily by inviting the parishioners to join you and the children in reciting the Lord's Prayer.

Thank the children for joining you and invite them to return to their seats.

Matthew 6:24-34

"So do not start worrying: 'Where will my food come from? or my drink? or my clothes?' Your Father in heaven knows that you need all these things." (Matthew 6:31, 32b, *Today's English Version*)

Summary

In today's reading from the Gospel of Matthew, Jesus urges us not to worry, but to trust God for life's necessities. In today's homily, children hear Jesus' words, then dispose of "worry stones."

Materials

Bible
small rocks, egg-sized or smaller, one per child
waste basket, trash can or heavy cloth bag
colorful artificial bird (available at craft stores)
colorful artificial flower

Homily

Invite the children to come forward for today's homily. Ask them to sit in a semicircle around you.

Ask the children:
- Who knows what it means to worry?
- What things do people worry about?
- What things do we worry about?

Note: The concept of *worry* may be too abstract for younger children. The related idea of *fear*, however, is not. If necessary, steer the discussion in the direction of fear:
- Sometimes we worry about things we are afraid of, like getting lost in a store or not getting a piece of cake when other people get one.
- What things are we sometimes afraid of?

Hand each child a rock. Explain:
- Let's call these rocks our "worry stones" (or "fear stones").
- Let's pretend each of our rocks is really all of our worries (and fears) rolled up into one little stone.
- Hold on to your worry (and fear) stone as Jesus talks to us about worrying in today's gospel story.

Hold the Bible open to the Gospel of Matthew as you tell today's story:

Jesus and his friends sat in the shade of an old tree. Jesus closed his eyes and listened as his friends talked. One woman

said, "I worry about whether I'll have enough food for my children. We've always had enough, but what if one day it's gone?"

"I know what you mean," said the man seated next to her. "I feel that way about my clothes. This is a great coat, but what will I do when it wears out? Where will I find another?"

"Yes," said another woman. "And what about this dry spell? If we don't have rain soon, we'll have no water to drink! That worries me, too!"

Jesus listened and thought to himself, My friends worry a lot. They worry so much that they've forgotten to enjoy God.

Jesus opened his eyes and said to his friends, "Don't be so worried about the food and drink you need in order to stay alive, or about clothes for you body."

Jesus looked up into the tree. "See the bird on that branch?" he said. *(Hold up bird.)* "Do you think this bird worries about what it's going to eat or whether it has water to drink? No! *God* takes care of this bird. And God loves you even more than God loves this bird. God will take care of you too.

"See these flowers?" Jesus asked. *(Hold up flower.)* "Do you think this flower worries about it clothes? No! *God* takes care of this flower, giving it the most beautiful clothes in the world. God loves you even more than God loves this flower. God will take care of you too.

Jesus' friends smiled. Maybe they didn't need to worry so much after all.

Ask:
- Who still has their worry (and fear) stones?
- Maybe we don't need to worry (and fear) so much either.
- Let's throw our worries (and fears) away.

Invite children to toss their stones into the waste basket, trash can or bag. Some children may wish to keep their stones; allow them to do so.

Prayer
- Dear God, thanks for taking good care of us. Help us to worry less and trust you more. *Amen.*

Thank the children for joining you and invite them to return to their seats.

36

■　■　■　■　■

Matthew 7:24-27

**"Anyone who hears these words
of mine and obeys them is like a
wise man who built his house
on rock." (Matthew 7:24,
Today's English Version)**

Summary

In this reading from the Gospel of
Matthew, Jesus explains that listening to and following him is like
building a secure house on a solid
foundation. In today's homily, children participate in the telling of
the story by building houses of
both newspaper and bricks.

Materials

Bible
2 large tubs or basins
several large containers of water
old newspapers
wooden blocks or concrete blocks
  or bricks

Homily

Invite the children to come forward for today's homily. Ask them
to sit in a semicircle around you.

Hold the Bible open to the Gospel
of Matthew as you tell today's
story:

**Jesus sat on a hillside talking
to some of his friends. They all
felt warm and relaxed in the
sunshine. A breeze brought
the scent of flowers and dried
grass.**

**Jesus had been talking to his
friends all day, teaching them
about God and love and the
Kingdom of heaven. He wondered if they had been listening. Do you ever wonder if people listen to you? Jesus did too,
so he told his friends this story:**

**"Once there was a man and a
woman. Each one wanted to
build a house.**

**"One of the two house-builders
was wise: she knew her house
would never last unless she
built it on solid ground, far
from the river, so that floods
and winds and rains and earthquakes could never move it.
She took her time, looking and
looking until she found just**

37

the right spot. It was far from town, so she had to walk a long ways, carrying all the materials up a long hill. She didn't mind, though, because she wanted a house that would last and last." *(Enlist the aid of the children in building a sturdy house of blocks or bricks inside one of the tubs or basins.)*

Jesus continued: "The other house builder was foolish: he wanted to build his house *fast* and *easy*. He built it on the first place he found, close to town, right next to the river. The ground was sandy and kinda wet, and it was at the bottom of a hill, but at least he wouldn't have to work hard." *(Enlist the aid of the children in building a flimsy house of a few sheets of old newspaper in the other tub or basin.)*

Jesus continued: "Well, not too long after the man and the woman both finished their houses, the rain started falling, and the wind started blowing, and the river started flooding. It was a terrible storm that went on for days. *(Pour water over both structures. Pour enough water over the newspaper house to collapse it.)*

"When the storm ended, the woman at the top of the hill looked out her window, and way at the bottom of the hill, right where the man's house used to be, was...*nothing*!"

What do you supposed happened to the man's house?

Jesus was done with his story. He sat quietly for a minute before he said, "If you listen to what I say and do it, you're like the woman who built her house on solid ground. If you don't listen to me and don't do what I say, you're like the man who built his house on the sandy ground."

Ask the children:
■ What things do you think Jesus wants us to do?

Prayer

■ Dear Jesus, Help us to listen to what you say. Help us to follow you. *Amen.*

Thank the children for joining you and invite them to return to their seats.

■ ■ ■ ■ ■

Matthew 9:9-13

Jesus left that place, and as he walked along, he saw a tax collector, named Matthew, sitting in his office. He said to him, "Follow me." (Matthew 9:9, *Today's English Version*)

Summary

In this reading from the Gospel of Matthew, Jesus calls Matthew to follow him, despite the prejudice and criticism of the Pharisees. In today's homily, children roleplay both rejection and acceptance as they participate in today's story.

Materials

Bible

Homily

Invite the children to come forward for today's homily. Ask them to sit in a semicircle around you.

Hold the Bible open to the Gospel of Matthew as you tell today's story:

One day, as Jesus was walking along, he saw a tax collector sitting in his office. The man's name was Matthew. Jesus said to Matthew, "Come with me. I want you to be one of my special friends, one of my disciples."

Matthew got right up and followed Jesus.

Matthew was happy to be following Jesus. But some people were very *unhappy* that Matthew followed Jesus. These people didn't like Matthew because he was a tax collector. They didn't think tax collectors were nice people. They wouldn't talk to tax collectors. They wouldn't invite tax collectors over for dinner. They wouldn't let their children play with the children of tax collectors.

Back in the days of Jesus, tax collectors were *outcasts*. Have you ever felt like an outcast? Have you ever felt rejected? Have you ever felt lonely? That's how Matthew felt...until Jesus asked him to come along with him.

People asked Jesus, "Why do you eat with people like Matthew? It's disgusting!"

39

Jesus said to them, "I came to be friends with outcasts. I came to eat with them, to hold them, to laugh with them, to heal them and to love them."

Ask the children to spread out at the front of the church, each child sitting alone apart from any others. When all children have found new spots to sit, say to them all:

■ Imagine you're Matthew, all alone, with no friends to play with, no family to talk to, nowhere to go.

■ You feel very sad and lonely, until something wonderful happens. Jesus comes and asks you to join him.

■ You pretend to be Matthew, sitting there all alone, and I'll pre- tend to be Jesus. Wait there until I come for you.

Go from child to child saying some- thing like "Matthew, come with me. I want you to be one of my special friends, one of my disci- ples." Have the children you gather accompany you as you move to and invite the next child. Gathered chil- dren can extend the invitation to each new *Matthew*.

Prayer

■ Jesus, thank you for loving and never rejecting the outcasts. Thanks for loving me. *Amen.*

Thank the children for joining you and invite them to return to their seats.

Matthew 9:35–10:8

Jesus called his twelve disciples together and gave them authority to drive out evil spirits and to heal every disease and every sickness. (Matthew 10:1, *Today's English Version*)

Summary

In this reading from the Gospel of Matthew, Jesus, seeing the need to bring hope and healing to the people, commissions his disciples to bring the Kingdom of heaven to the people of Israel. In today's homily, children hear the story of the disciples' commissioning, then review the names of the disciples with a song.

Materials

Bible

Homily

Invite the children to come forward for today's homily. Ask them to sit in a semicircle around you.

Hold the Bible open to the Gospel of Matthew as you tell today's story:

Jesus walked and Jesus talked, all through the land of Israel. Jesus walked near and far to heal the sick. Jesus talked to tell good news to the sad. "Rejoice!" said Jesus. "God loves you. God's kingdom is near."

But the more Jesus walked and the more Jesus talked, the more he saw people who needed him: people who were sick, people who were sad, people who were worried.

"I feel so sorry for these people," said Jesus. "How can I help even more of them?"

Jesus called together his friends. "Look," said Jesus. "There are so many people who need help and so few workers to help. Will you help?"

"Yes," said the twelve friends of Jesus. And these were the names of the twelve: *Peter* and *Andrew*, *James* and *John*, *Philip* and *Bartholomew*, *Thomas* and *Matthew*, *James* and *Thaddeus*, *Simon* and *Judas*. "We'll help you," said the twelve.

"Good!" said Jesus. "Then go to all the people of Israel. Heal the

sick. Raise the dead. And tell everyone, 'God loves you. The kingdom of heaven is near'"

Teach the children the following song, sung to the tune of "This Old Man." Invite children (and the parishioners!) to join in as they pick up the tune. You, of course, will have to sing the second line of each verse, which identifies that verse's disciple. You might also invite children to hold up the appropriate number of fingers for each verse of the song, adding their feet for the final two verses (11 and 12).

1. Jesus Christ, he called one:
    "Matthew, come and be my son."
    Matthew followed Jesus from that very day.
    Follow Jesus Christ today.

2. Jesus Christ, he called two:
    "Peter, be my son so true."
    Peter followed Jesus from that very day.
    Follow Jesus Christ today.

3. Jesus Christ, he called three:
    "Andrew, will you follow me?"
    Andrew...

4. Jesus Christ, he called four:
    "James, I need one helper more."
    James...

5. Jesus Christ, he called five:
    "John, I'll make you feel alive."
    John...

6. Jesus Christ, he called six:
    "Philip, bring your walking stick."
    Philip...

7. Jesus Christ, he called seven:
    "Bartholomew, you've a home in heaven."
    Bartholomew...

8. Jesus Christ, he called eight:
    "Thomas, come! It's getting late."
    Thomas...

9. Jesus Christ, he called nine:
    "James, come be a child of mine."
    James...

10. Jesus Christ, he called ten:
    "Thaddeus, come and be my friend."
    Thaddeus...

11. Jesus Christ, he called eleven:
    "Simon, follow me to heaven."
    Simon...

12. Jesus Christ, he called twelve:
    "Judas, offer me yourself."
    Judas...

Prayer

■ Thank you, Jesus, for calling all of us here today—children and adults—to be your disciples, too. *Amen.*

Thank the children for joining you and invite them to return to their seats.

■ ■ ■ ■ ■

Matthew 10:
16-20, 28-31

"So do not be afraid; you are worth much more than many sparrows!" (Matthew 10:31, *Today's English Version*)

Summary

In this reading from the Gospel of Matthew, Jesus assures us that God's loving care for the birds is far surpassed by God's love for us. In today's homily, children hear the story from the gospel reading, share a few "trouble stories" and hear reassurances that God cares for them in their troubles.

Materials

Bible
bird picture or figurine

Homily

Invite the children to come forward for today's homily. Ask them to sit in a semicircle around you.

Hold the Bible open to the Gospel of Matthew as you tell today's story:

"What do you think?" asked Peter. "Will we be able to do the job Jesus wants us to do? Will we be able to bring people into God's kingdom?"

"Well," said his brother, Andrew, "we are grown men. We know how to fish. We know how to take care of a boat. But this new job that Jesus has given us is different. I don't know what it will be like at all."

Jesus heard Peter and Andrew. He came to sit down next to them. "You're worried about what your new job will be like," said Jesus. He put one arm around Peter's shoulder and one around Andrew's. "Well, there will be good days when you see people happy to come to God's kingdom."

Peter and Andrew smiled at this, but Jesus went on. "You will have bad days, too. You will have enemies who will bring you many troubles."

"Troubles!" said Andrew. "What will I do when troubles come?"

"There are some troubles," said Jesus, "that we can hardly stand. We only get through them because we know that God sees us and cares so much about us."

Just then two sparrows flew down nearby and hopped on the ground, pecking for seed. Jesus pointed to them and said,

"When troubles come, remember the sparrows."

"Sparrows!" sputtered Peter. "Sparrows are no help to people in trouble!"

"Listen to Jesus," said Andrew quietly. And Peter listened.

"God sees and cares about each little sparrow that looks for food — or runs from a cat." Now Jesus smiled at the two brothers. *(Look into each child's eyes as you say with emphasis:)* "And you are worth much more to God than any sparrow."

Cradle the bird picture or figurine in your hand. Ask children to think about troubles, big and small. Briefly share a trouble of your own that you think appropriate for the children to hear. After you share, hold the bird close to your heart and say, "I'm glad God sees and cares about me in my troubles."

Pass the bird around the circle. Emphasize that children only share if they want to. After each story, say, "I'm glad God sees and cares about (*child's name*) in her (*or his*) trouble."

Prayer

■ Jesus, you say to each one of us, "Do not be afraid; you are worth much more than many sparrows!" Thank you, Jesus. *Amen.*

Thank the children for joining you and invite them to return to their seats.

■ ■ ■ ■ ■

Matthew 10:40-42

"You can be sure that whoever gives even a drink of cold water to one of the least of these my followers because he is my follower, will certainly receive a reward." (Matthew 10:42, *Today's English Version*)

Summary

In this reading from the Gospel of Matthew, Jesus explains that those who welcome his followers, welcome him. In today's homily, children hear the gospel story, then welcome Jesus in one another by sharing cups of cold water.

Materials

Bible
small paper cups, 2 per child
several plastic pitchers of water

Homily

Invite the children to come forward for today's homily. Ask them to sit in a semicircle around you.

Hold the Bible open to the Gospel of Matthew as you tell today's story:

Jesus walked for miles and miles at a time. He healed a blind man's eyes. He gave life to a dying girl. He made a sick man well. He stopped a woman's bleeding.

Now you might think that with all this work Jesus always

hurried, never sat down, never rested, but no. He spent quiet hours praying. He spent friendly hours talking with his disciples.

Once he said to them, "Whoever welcomes you, welcomes me."

"That sounds easy," said James. He turned to Peter and gave Peter a hug. "Welcome, Jesus," said James. (Turn to and hug two or three children seated nearby, saying, as you hug each, "Welcome, Jesus.")

Jesus laughed. "That's right," he said. "You share in my work. I share in your life. When you go out, you do my work. When people see your work, they see me. When people welcome you, they welcome me."

"Even if they just give a hug, like James?" said Peter?

"Even if they just give a cup of cold water," said Jesus. "You can be sure that if someone stops to give even a drink of water to you because you are my follower, the person who gives will certainly be rewarded."

Pour a cup of water and hand it to the child next to you to take a sip. As the child sips, say, "Welcome, Jesus."

Ask that child to repeat your actions and the words for the next child. Continue until the last child has poured and offered water to you and welcomed you as Jesus.

Then pour a second cup of water for each child. (Older children can help younger children with this.) Ask the children to take these second cups carefully into the congregation to give to others as they say to them, "Welcome, Jesus."

Regather the children for the prayer.

Prayer

■ Dear God, it's wonderful for us to be here, in a place where Jesus is welcome and where we are welcome. Thank you. *Amen*.

Thank the children for joining you and invite them to return to their seats.

46

■ ■ ■ ■ ■

Matthew 11:2-6

"Tell us," they asked Jesus, "are you the one John said was going to come, or should we expect someone else?" Jesus answered, "Go back and tell John what you are hearing and seeing..." (Matthew 11:3-4, *Today's English Version***)**

Summary

In this reading from the Gospel of Matthew, John the Baptist sends his followers to ask Jesus if Jesus is, indeed, the long-awaited Messiah. In today's homily, children hear today's gospel story and carry to the church Jesus' message to John, "Jesus is God's Son!"

Materials

Bible

Homily

Invite the children to come forward for today's homily. Ask them to sit in a semicircle around you.

Hold the Bible open to the Gospel of Matthew as you tell today's story:

John the Baptist did God's work for many years. "God's Son is coming!" John told God's people. God's Son will bring peace wherever there's hurt. God's Son will bring good news to God's people."

John also told people how to get ready for God's Son. "Stop hurting; help one another instead," said John. "Don't steal. If you have two shirts, give one away to the person who has none."

The people loved John, because John was fearless and brave. When the king broke the law, John was not afraid to go to the king and say, "Even if you are the king, you are supposed to obey. You are doing wrong."

The king put John into prison. John never left the prison again. In the prison, John prayed, "God, let your Son come soon. Let your Son bring good news to all your people."

John's friends came to see John in prison. John and his friends talked together, cried together and prayed together. One day, a friend said, "God's Son is here! God's Son is Jesus!"

"How do I know?" asked John. "How can I know God's Son is here?"

John sent friends to Jesus.

"John wants to know: are you really God's Son?" the friends asked. "Or do we have to wait longer for God's Son to come?"

"Go tell John what you see and hear," said Jesus. "I can make blind people see; I can make crippled people walk; I can make sick people well. I can even make the dead live again. I bring peace wherever there's hurt. I bring good news to God's people."

"Then are you really God's Son?" asked one of John's friends.

Jesus looked at the friend and said, "Happy is anyone who believes in me."

Then the friends ran back to John to tell him all that Jesus had said.

After the story, ask:
- What did you hear about John the Baptist in today's story? *(John the Baptist was in prison, told people to get ready for Jesus, sent friends to find out if God's Son was here, etc.)*
- What did you hear about Jesus in today's story? *(Jesus said he could make blind people see, crippled people walk, dead people live, etc.)*
- Who could we tell that Jesus really is God's Son?
- Who could we tell that Jesus heals people?
- Who could we tell that Jesus can make dead people live again?

Solicit many answers from children for these final three questions. End by looking out toward the parishioners and saying:
- I see lots of people seated right here today.
- We could tell them that Jesus really is God's Son. Shall we do that?

As you dismiss the children, send them back to their seats with this final challenge:
- On the way back to your family, tell at least five other people, "Jesus is God's Son!"

■ ■ ■ ■ ■

Matthew 11:28-30

"Come to me, all of you who are tired from carrying heavy loads, and I will give you rest." (Matthew 11:28, *Today's English Version***)**

Summary

In this reading from the Gospel of Matthew, Jesus invites us to share our burdens with him. In today's homily children hear the story from today's gospel, then learn and sing a song about Jesus, their helper.

Materials

Bible

Homily

Invite the children to come forward for today's homily. Ask them to sit in a semicircle around you.

Hold the Bible open to the Gospel of Matthew as you tell today's story:

Once a friend of Jesus, named Peter, said, "How I wish I had a friend who could help me keep my temper."

"Let me be that friend," said Jesus.

A woman named Mary Magdalene said, "I feel like seven demons are living inside me and making me do crazy things. How I wish I had a friend who would help me get rid of the demons!"

"Let me be that friend," said Jesus.

A man with terrible sores on his skin said, "How I wish my skin were smooth and well. I need a friend who can make me well."

"Let me be that friend," said Jesus.

Children who had no books— and certainly no television — said to themselves, "Oh, how we wish we had a grown-up friend who would tell us stories."

"Let me be that friend," said Jesus.

To all these people—and to you!—Jesus says, "Come to me. Let me be your helper and your friend."

Teach the children the song, "I Have a Helper," sung to the tune of "B-I-N-G-O":

I have a helper and a friend,
I know his name is Jesus.
J-E-S-U-S,
J-E-S-U-S,
J-E-S-U-S,
I know his name is Jesus.

Repeat the song several times with the children, then invite the parishioners to join you for several more renditions.

Prayer

■ Thank you, Jesus, for being our helper. *Amen.*

Thank the children for joining you and invite them to return to their seats.

Matthew 12:46-50

Jesus answered, "Who is my mother? Who are my brothers?" Then he pointed to his disciples and said, "Look! Here are my mother and my brothers!" (Matthew 12:48-49, *Today's English Version*)

Summary

In this reading from the Gospel of Matthew, Jesus explains that those who do the will of God are members of his family. In today's homily, children first hear this story, then learn and sing a song about God's family.

Materials

Bible

optional:

accompanist to play the music for "I Have a Family," printed below

Note: There are two ways to use the song "I Have a Family" in today's homily:

■ Teach the children (and the parishioners) the chorus. Sing the chorus only several times.

■ Or, **before the homily**, invite a volunteer (adult or an older child) to learn the two verses of the song. In the homily, teach the children (and the parishioners) the chorus only. Have the children (and the parishioners) sing the chorus and the volunteer sing the verses.

Homily

Invite the children to come forward for today's homily. Ask the children to sit in a semicircle around you.

If you wish, begin the homily by discussing:

■ What is a family?

■ What do you like best about your family?

■ Jesus once said a surprising thing about his family, and that's the story I want to tell you today.

Hold the Bible open to the Gospel of Matthew as you tell today's story:

Jesus' mother and brothers arrive at the house. Inside the house, Jesus is teaching. But the house is so crowded that Jesus' mother and brothers cannot step inside.

Jesus' mother cranes her neck to see her son, but there are too many people in the way. One of Jesus' brothers tries to push between two women, but they won't let him by.

"So many people!" Jesus' mother says.

"So crowded!" his brothers say.

The people pass a message to Jesus: "Your mother and brothers are outside on the porch. They want to see you."

"My mother?" Jesus asks. "My brothers? Let me tell you something." He waves his hand toward the people crowding around him, women and men, girls and boys, moms and dads, grandmothers and grandfathers, sick people and well people, tall people and short people...all the people he can see, people sitting on chairs and on the floor, people standing in doorways and windows. "All of these people are my sisters and brothers, my mothers and fathers. You are all my family."

Jesus says to each one of us (indicate each child), "You are my family."

Jesus says to all of us (indicate the entire congregation), "You are my family."

Teach and sing "I Have a Family," printed below.

Prayer

■ We are glad, Jesus, to be your brothers and sisters. Thanks for making God's family such a big, wonderful family. *Amen.*

Thank the children for joining you and invite them to return to their seats.

I HAVE A FAMILY

Words and music by Pamela L. Hughes

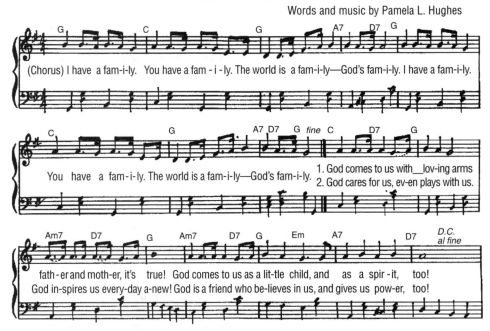

(Chorus) I have a fam-i-ly. You have a fam - i - ly. The world is a fam-i-ly—God's fam-i-ly. I have a fam-i-ly.

You have a fam-i-ly. The world is a fam-i-ly—God's fam-i-ly.

1. God comes to us with__lov-ing arms
2. God cares for us, ev-en plays with us.

fath - er and moth-er, it's true! God comes to us as a lit-tle child, and as a spir - it, too!
God in-spires us every-day a-new! God is a friend who be-lieves in us, and gives us pow-er, too!

■ ■ ■ ■ ■

Matthew 13:1-9

He used parables to tell them many things. Once there was a man who went out to sow grain. (Matthew 13:3, *Today s English Version*)

Summary

In this reading from the Gospel of Matthew, Jesus tells the parable of the seed sown in different types of soil. In today's homily, children hear this story and express their knowledge of and appreciation for growing things.

Materials

Bible
"God Makes Things Grow" poster
   (see **before the homily** note)

Before the homily create a "God Makes Things Grow" poster:
■ Write the title *God Makes Things Grow* in large letters across the top of a large sheet of poster board.
■ On the poster board draw or glue pictures of things that grow, for example, flowers and trees; puppies, kittens and other animals; babies and children; etc. Sources of pictures include stickers and pictures cut from magazines.

Homily

Invite the children to come forward for today's homily. Ask them to sit in a semicircle around you.

Show children the "God Makes Things Grow" poster prepared **before the homily**. Invite them to name things that grow, including those pictured on the poster. Say:
■ Let's listen to a story that Jesus told about something that grows.

Hold the Bible open to the Gospel of Matthew as you tell today's story:

Once there was a farmer...a farmer with seeds...a farmer with seeds in the spring...a farmer with seeds in the spring and a field in which to plant them.

The farmer scattered the seeds in the field...seeds to the right ...seeds to the left...seeds in front of him...seeds behind him.

Some seeds fell beside a path and stayed on top of the dirt. Birds flew by and saw these seeds...pecked at these seeds ...ate these seeds until not one was left.

53

Some of the seeds from the farmer's hand fell on rocky ground. The birds didn't find them, so the seeds had time to grow...time to open...time to put out tiny roots...time to grow little stems. But then those tiny roots bumped into rocks. Without big roots, the tiny plants couldn't grow. Soon not one was left.

Some of the farmer's seeds fell into dirt. The birds didn't find them, there was no rocky ground, so they grew. But...so did weeds. The seeds grew fast. The weeds grew faster. Soon not one seed was left.

But some of the farmer's seeds fell into good, rich soil. The birds didn't find them there; no rocky ground was there; no weeds grew there. The seeds opened...the seeds grew...the seeds made more seeds. Thirty times as many seeds! Sixty times as many seeds! A hundred times as many seeds!

If you wish, ask the children:
■ What's your favorite growing thing?
■ Let's thank God for all good growing things.

Prayer

■ Thank you, God, for all that grows, including each child here. Thanks, God, for sending Jesus to tell us stories about growing things. *Amen.*

Thank the children for joining you and invite them to return to their seats.

■ ■ ■ ■ ■

Matthew 13:24-30

Jesus told them another parable: "The Kingdom of heaven is like this. A man sowed good seed in his field." (Matthew 13:24, *Today's English Version*)

Summary

In this reading from the Gospel of Matthew, Jesus compares God's kingdom to a field of plants struggling to survive in the midst of weeds. In today's homily, children participate in the telling of this story by pretending to be tiny seeds and healthy young plants.

Materials

Bible

Homily

Invite the children to come forward for today's homily. Ask them to sit in a semicircle around you.

As you tell today's story, encourage the children to join you in the motions.

Hold the Bible open to the Gospel of Matthew as you tell today's story:

One warm, sunny day Jesus planted seeds. Jesus dug little holes for the seeds *(dig a hole)*, put the seeds in the holes *(plant the seeds)* and gently covered them up *(pat the dirt)*.

"Grow, little seeds," said Jesus. "I will take good care of you so that you can grow big and strong."

The little seeds squiggled their toes deep into the dirt. *(Squiggle your toes.)* They reached way up high until they could poke their heads out, into the light and the air. *(Sit up very straight, lift your head and smile.)* "We're growing fast!" said the seeds.

But something else was growing fast. Weeds! Big weeds! Strong weeds! Mean weeds! *(Flex muscles and look mean.)*

"Ouch," said the little plants to the weeds, "You're squishing us!" *(Curl yourself up into a tight ball.)*

Now when Jesus came to see his seeds, he saw those weeds growing, too.

"Help, Jesus!" the little plants said, "These weeds are big! These weeds are strong! These weeds are mean!"

But Jesus said, "I can't pull out the weeds *(shake your head no)* or I might pull *you* out, too. So the weeds will stay. But don't worry: I'll take care of you. You'll grow up big and strong, too." *(Flex muscles and smile.)*

And they did! The seeds grew. *(Raise left hand to show growth.)* But Jesus threw all the weeds away. *(Crumple right hand and make a tossing motion.)*

Prayer

■ Thank you, God, for seeds that grow and for people who care for growing seeds. Thank you, God, for these growing children. Thank you, God, for Jesus, who cares for these growing children. *Amen.*

Thank the children for joining you and invite them to return to their seats.

56

■ ■ ■ ■ ■

Matthew 13:44

"The Kingdom of heaven is like this. A man happens to find a treasure hidden in a field. He covers it up again, and is so happy that he goes and sells everything he has, and then goes back and buys that field." (Matthew 13:44, *Today's English Version*)

Summary

In this reading from the Gospel of Matthew, Jesus compares God's kingdom to an inestimable treasure, worth sacrificing all. In today's homily, children make play-dough "treasures," then listen to the telling of today's story.

Materials

Bible
play dough (**Note:** You can make your own play dough by mixing together 1-1/2 cups flour, 1/2 cup salt, 1/2 cup water and 1/4 cup oil. Knead well. Use food coloring to tint the dough. Store in plastic containers.)

Homily

Invite the children to come forward for today's homily. Ask them to sit in a semicircle around you.

Give each child a small lump of play dough. Explain:
■ Use your play dough to make

something special for today's story: a treasure, a toy or any other special belonging.
■ Tell us what you're making as you work.

Spend only a minute or two discussing children's treasures as they work, then ask them to put their treasures on the floor in front of them as you tell the story. Hold the Bible open to the Gospel of Matthew as you continue:

Once day a man goes walking, up hill and down, when he comes to a field filled with bright flowers. But as he walks across the field, he stumbles.

He looks down. There he sees the edge of a large pottery jar, jutting out of the ground.

57

What can this be? he wonders.

He kneels beside it and brushes away the dirt. The mouth of the jar is stuffed with an old rag. The man pulls out the rag— and catches his breath. Inside are golden coins, more than he has ever seen in his life. Here and there, many-colored jewels sparkle in the sun.

Slowly the man stuffs the rag back into the jar. What should I do? he thinks. I cannot take the jar. This field does not belong to me.

He walks back to town and goes to the owner of the field, a rich man. "What do you want for that field?" says the man to the owner. The owner names a price far beyond what the field is really worth—if not for the secret hidden in it.

The man does not hesitate. He runs home. He gathers everything he has: *(Name the chil-dren's play-dough treasures as items that the man sells.)* He sells all these treasures so that he can buy the field. Then he takes the money to the owner and buys the field.

The secret treasure is his!

If you wish, ask the children:
■ What do you think the best treasure in all the world might be?
■ What treasure do you think God wants to give us?

Prayer

■ Thank you, God, for the treasure of these children: *(If possible, name each child.)* Amen.

Thank the children for joining you and invite them to return to their seats.

Matthew 14:13-21

He ordered the people to sit down on the grass; then he took the five loaves and the two fish, looked up to heaven, and gave thanks to God. (Matthew 14:19a, *Today's English Version*)

Summary

In this reading from the Gospel of Matthew, Jesus feeds thousands of people with only two fish and five loaves of bread. In today's homily, children listen to the story, then retell the story by singing a simple song.

Materials

Bible
chalkboard and chalk or newsprint
   and marker

Homily

Invite the children to come forward for today's homily. Ask them to be seated in a semicircle around you.

Hold the Bible open to the Gospel of Matthew as you tell today's story. Use the motions indicated in italics:

Jesus is coming! Let's walk to the big hill to see Jesus! *("Walk" hands on floor.)*

Oh, that was a long walk! But look at all the people who are here. *(Point to the parishioners.)*

Oh, those are so many people. Now Jesus is talking. Let's listen to what Jesus says. *(Cup hand behind ear.)* What do *you* think Jesus is talking about? *(Allow children to answer before continuing.)*

Oh, that was a long talk! I like to listen to Jesus, but I'm hungry. *(Rub tummy.)* Are you hungry? Are *they* hungry? *(Point to parishioners.)*

But we don't want to leave Jesus. What will we do? *(Hold up hands in puzzlement.)*

Look, a little child is giving Jesus a basket.

Look, Jesus is opening the basket. He's taking out bread and fish.

Five loaves of bread? *(Hold up five fingers.)* Two fish? *(Hold*

59

up two fingers.) **What good are those with all these people?** *(Point to parishioners.)*

Jesus is holding up the food. Jesus says, "Thank you, God." Jesus is breaking the bread.

Look! Here comes some of the bread for us. Let's eat. *(Pretend to eat.)* **There's bread for you ...bread for me...bread for all these people.** *(Point to parishioners.)*

Jesus fed us all! With just two fish and five loaves of bread.

If you wish, discuss with the children:
■ Jesus gave people bread and fish to eat.
■ What food would you like to thank God for today?

Sing this song to the tune of "The Farmer in the Dell." Invite children to add motions as appropriate:

1. The people on the hill,
   The people on the hill,
   Heigh-ho, the derry-o,
   The people on the hill.

2. The people want to eat,
   The people want to eat,
   Heigh-ho, the derry-o,
   The people want to eat.

3. We have some bread and fish...

4. So Jesus takes the bread...

5. Then Jesus gives God thanks...

6. Then Jesus breaks the bread...

7. Then Jesus shares the food...

8. Now everyone is full...

Prayer

■ Dear God, thank you giving us food. Thank you for sending Jesus to give us what we need. *Amen.*

Thank the children for joining you and invite them to return to their seats.

■　■　■　■　■

Matthew 14:22-33

Between three and six o'clock in the morning Jesus came to the disciples, walking on the water. (Matthew 14:25; *Today's English Version*)

Summary

In this reading from the Gospel of Matthew, Jesus saves Peter from sinking in the waters of the sea. In today's homily, children discuss their fears and help tell today's story in musical form.

Materials

Bible
large sheet of poster board
felt marker

Homily

Invite the children to come forward for today's homily. Ask them to be seated in a semicircle around you.

Begin the homily by asking:
- What things scare us? *(As children offer answers, draw or write their fears on the poster board.)*
- What do we do when we are afraid?
- Once Peter—one of Jesus' disciples—was afraid, too. Will you help me tell the story of Peter? Today's story is a song, and I'll teach it to you.

Teach children the following song to the tune of "The Wheels on the Bus." Invite them to do the motions

with you. Have the Bible open beside you to the Gospel of Matthew:

O Jesus on the sea goes walk,
   walk, walk;
Walk, walk, walk;
Walk, walk, walk.
O Jesus on the sea goes walk,
   walk, walk.
Jesus our Lord.

("Walk" your fingers in your hands.)

Now Peter in the sea goes
   splash, splash, splash;
Splash, splash, splash;
Splash, splash, splash.
Now Peter in the sea goes
   splash, splash, splash.
Jesus our Lord.

(Slap thighs with hands.)

O Peter in the sea cries, "Help!
   Help! Help!
Help! Help! Help!
Help! Help! Help!"
O Peter in the sea cries, "Help!

Help! Help!"
Jesus our Lord.

(Raise and wave arms.)

So Jesus holds out his hand,
    hand, hand.
Hand, hand, hand.
Hand, hand, hand.
So Jesus holds out his hand,
    hand, hand.
Jesus our Lord.

(Alternate and extend hands.)

Now Peter in the boat says,
    "Thanks! Thanks! Thanks!
Thanks! Thanks! Thanks!
Thanks! Thanks! Thanks!"
Now Peter in the boat says,
    "Thanks! Thanks! Thanks!"
Jesus our Lord.

(Fold hands in prayer.)

Refer to the chalkboard or newsprint on which your have drawn or written children's fears. Invite children to join you in a litany that calls on Jesus for help in scary times. Point to one of the fears identified on the poster, say:

■ From *(name fear)...*

Ask children to respond with:

■ Jesus, save us!

Repeat for additional fears drawn or written on chalkboard or newsprint. For example, the litany could begin in this way:

■ From big dogs that bite...
■ Jesus, save us!
■ From being left alone in the grocery store...
■ Jesus, save us!
■ From bullies at school...
■ Jesus, save us!

Prayer

■ Thank you, Jesus, for hearing Peter and helping him. Help us when we call on you too. *Amen.*

Thank the children for joining you and invite them to return to their seats.

Matthew 15:21-28

A Canaanite woman who lived in that region came to him, "Son of David!" she cried out. "Have mercy on me, sir! My daughter has a demon and is in a terrible condition." (Matthew 15:22, *Today's English Version*)

Summary

In this reading from the Gospel of Matthew, Jesus stops to heal the daughter of a Canaanite woman. In today's homily, children first identify God's "love of differences" as they observe the variety in God's created world, then hear a version of today's gospel story.

Materials

Bible

grocery bag containing 6 or more different pieces of fruit: grape, apple, banana, etc.

lidded box containing pictures of 6 or more animals (see **note** below)

Note: You could cut pictures of animals from magazines, or copy these simple drawings onto separate 8" x 11" sheets of paper:

Homily

Invite the children to come forward for today's homily. Ask them to be seated in a semicircle around you.

Peek inside the grocery bag, choose a piece of fruit, and give several clues about it. Slowly draw the piece of fruit out of the bag, encouraging the children to guess the fruit's name.

Sample clues:
- This fruit is round and red. You can eat its skin. Its name begins with an *a. (apple)*
- This fruit is long and skinny and yellow. You can't eat its skin. Its name begins with a *b. (banana)*

When all the fruit has been drawn form the bag, ask volunteers to help you hold up the fruit so all can see it (including the parishioners). Slowly say:

■ God must love differences to make so many different kinds of fruit.

Show the box and explain that you have pictures of different kinds of animals inside. Give clues for each animal, similar to the fruit clues.

Sample clues:

■ This animal has fur and is small enough to pick up. It's a pet for some people and its name begins with a *c.* The sound it makes is "meow." *(cat)*
■ This animal slithers. Some people keep one for a pet, but you usually find it outside. Its name begins with an *s* and it makes a hissing sound. *(snake)*

As with the fruit, ask volunteers to hold the pictures up so all can see. Say slowly:

■ God must love differences to make so many different kinds of animals.

Now ask 6-10 of the children to stand side by side in a line facing the parishioners. Say slowly:

■ God must love differences to make so many different kinds of people.
■ Let's listen to a story about the different kinds of people God loves.

Hold the Bible open to the Gospel of Matthew as you tell today's story.

Sometimes people who had ugly sores on their skin came to see Jesus.

Jesus said, "Come close! I love all kinds of people!"

How do you think the people with the sores felt? *(Pause for children's responses.)*

Sometimes children came to Jesus. They hoped he would hold them close and tell them stories.

Jesus said, "Yes, come to me! I love all kinds of people!"

How do you think the children felt? *(Pause for children's responses.)*

Once a woman from a foreign country came to see Jesus. She said, "I am not like you, Jesus, or like any of your friends, but I want you to make my daughter well."

Jesus said, "I love you and your daughter. I will make her well. I love all kinds of people."

How do you think the woman felt? *(Pause for children's responses.)*

Prayer

■ Thank you, God, for making us all different, each special, each unique. Help us to be proud of—and to learn from—the ways we are different. Thank you for loving all the differences you've created. *Amen.*

Thank the children for joining you and invite them to return to their seats.

■ ■ ■ ■ ■

Matthew 16:13-20

Jesus went to the territory near the town of Caesarea Philippi, where he asked his disciples, "Who do people say the Son of Man is?" Simon Peter answered, "You are the Messiah, the Son of the living God." (Matthew 16:13, 16, *Today's English Version*)

Summary

In this reading from the Gospel of Matthew, Jesus affirms Peter for declaring Jesus to be "the Messiah, the Son of the living God." In today's homily, children play a quick game of Who Am I?, then listen to today's story.

Materials

Bible

Homily

Invite the children to come forward for today's homily. Ask them to be seated in a semicircle around you.

Ask the children:
■ Who am I?

Be content with simple answers, especially from the youngest children, who will probably give only a name or your common title. Encourage several more answers: *woman* or *man, storyteller, singer, friend*, etc.

Lay your hand on a child nearby and ask the child to repeat the question:
■ Who am I?

Encourage the children to join you in answering the question. Repeat for more children—all the children, if the size of the group allows.

Say:
■ One day, Jesus asked just that question—and that's the story I want to tell you today.

Hold the Bible open to the Gospel of Matthew as you tell today's story:

One day as Jesus walked with his friends he said, "Who do people think I am?"

65

Andrew said, "Some say that you are a prophet, because you tell God's word."

Philip said, "Some say that you are Elijah, who died long ago."

James said, "Some say that you are John the Baptist, who was killed by bad king Herod. Some say that you have come back to life."

Jesus asked his disciples, "But you, who do you say that I am?"

Peter spoke up. "You are the One whom God has chosen. You are the Son of the living God."

"This is a happy day for you, Peter," said Jesus. "God has told you who I really am."

Ask the children:
■ Who do *you* think Jesus is?

Accept and affirm all of the children's answers.

Prayer

■ Thank you, God, for sending Jesus, the Messiah, your own Son. *Amen.*

Thank the children for joining you and invite them to return to their seats.

■ ■ ■ ■ ■

Matthew 16:21-27

From that time on Jesus began to say plainly to his disciples, "I must go to Jerusalem and suffer much from the elders, the chief priests, and the teachers of the Law. I will be put to death, but three days later I will be raised to life." (Matthew 16:21, *Today's English Version***)**

Summary

In this reading from the Gospel of Matthew, Jesus predicts his approaching death and resurrection. In today's homily, children identify both sad and happy times in their lives, then hear today's gospel story.

Materials

Bible
Happy Times and *Sad Times* posters (see **note** below)

Note: Before the homily prepare two posters. On one poster draw a smiling face; title this first poster *Happy Times*. On the other poster draw a sad face; title this second poster *Sad Times*.

Homily

Invite the children to come forward for today's homily. Ask them to be seated in a semicircle around you.

Show children the *Happy Times* poster. Invite children to share

happy times in their lives from the past week.

After six to ten children have shared stories, show children the *Sad Times* poster. Invite children to share sad times in their lives from the past week.

After several children have shared stories, say:
■ Jesus' friends had many happy times with Jesus. *(Use some of the ideas shared by children, saying, for example, that Jesus and his friends would share favorite foods or play favorite games.)*
■ Jesus' friends had sad times with Jesus, too.

Hold the Bible open to the Gospel of Matthew as you tell today's story:

Jesus and his good friends were walking and talking. It was just getting dark; the air felt cool and dry. From the top of a nearby tree, doves cooed

softly to each other, preparing for sleep.

Jesus' friends were tired; they'd been walking all day. They had talked to people about God's love. They had healed people who were sick. They had listened to Jesus teach.

Before they stopped for the night, Jesus had one more thing to tell them. A sad thing. A thing they did not want to hear.

Jesus took a deep breath. "Soon I will do a hard thing," he said. "I will die on a cross."

"No!" say Jesus' friends, their eyes big. They felt frightened. "We don't want you to die!"

"Don't be afraid," says Jesus. "God loves me. God will help me do this hard thing."

"But if you die, that will be a very sad time!"

"I will die," said Jesus, "and that *will* be a very sad time. But there will be another time, soon after that—a happy time. Soon after I die, I will come back to life."

Sad time. Happy time. Jesus' friends struggled to understand.

But over and over they kept thinking of Jesus words: "God will help me do this hard thing."

They knew God would help them through the sad times, too.

Prayer

■ Jesus, you had happy times, just like us. You had sad times, just like us. Thank you for being close to us at *all* times, happy and sad. *Amen.*

Thank the children for joining you and invite them to return to their seats.

■ ■ ■ ■ ■

Matthew 17:1-9

As they looked on, a change came over Jesus: his face was shining like the sun, and his clothes were dazzling white. (Matthew 17:2, *Today's English Version***)**

Summary

In this reading from the Gospel of Matthew, Jesus is transfigured on the mountaintop, and a voice announces that he is God's dear Son. In today's homily, children participate in the telling of this story.

Materials

Bible
2 Jesus puppets (see **note** below)
small blanket
cloud shape cut from thin cardboard and covered with foil

Note: Before the homily prepare two Jesus puppets:
■ Make two photocopies of the Jesus figure printed on the next page.
■ Paste the photocopies to thin cardboard or heavy paper to stiffen them. Cut out both figures.
■ Color *one* of the figures.
■ Tape or glue each figure to its own tongue depressor or frozen treat stick.
■ Cover the uncolored figure with aluminum foil.

Homily

Invite the children to come forward for today's homily. Ask them to be seated in a semicircle around you.

Mound the blanket in front of you in the shape of a mountain. Place the Bible beside you, open to the Gospel of Matthew as you tell today's story:

One day Jesus takes Peter, James and John up a high mountain. (*Walk Jesus puppet up the blanket "mountain."*)

"No one else is here," says Jesus. "I want to pray for awhile."

It's nighttime, so Peter, James and John fall asleep. (*Encourage children to close their eyes, pretending to sleep.*) When they awake, they look at Jesus. (*Bring out foil-covered puppet.*)

They can't believe what they see! Jesus looks so different! His face shines as bright as the sun! His clothes are dazzling white!

Even though it's still night, they see a bright, shining cloud in the sky above them. (*Bring out foil-covered cloud shape.*)

Peter, James and John are afraid. "What is that?" they say.

They hear a voice coming from the bright cloud. It says, "This is my Son, Jesus. I am happy with him. Listen to him!"

Peter, James and John are so afraid that they fall on the ground and put their hands over their heads. *(Encourage children to cover their faces. Put away the foil-covered puppet and bring out the plain puppet.)*

Then Jesus touches each friend. *(If possible, touch each child with the plain puppet.)* "Get up," he says. "Don't be afraid."

They get up. There is Jesus, just as he always is. No more shining face. No more dazzling robes. Just Jesus, their old friend.

Then Jesus, Peter, James and John all climb back down the mountain together. *(Walk puppet back down the mountain.)*

Discuss with the children:
■ How did Peter, James and John see Jesus in today's story?
■ Imagine you saw Jesus this week.
  — Where might he be?
  — What do you think he'd look like?
■ What would you say to Jesus if you saw him?

Prayer

In prayer, direct to Jesus some of the comments and questions that the children offered in response to the final question in the homily.

Close by praying:
■ Thank you, God, for the wonderful change in Jesus. *Amen.*

Thank the children for joining you and invite them to return to their seats.

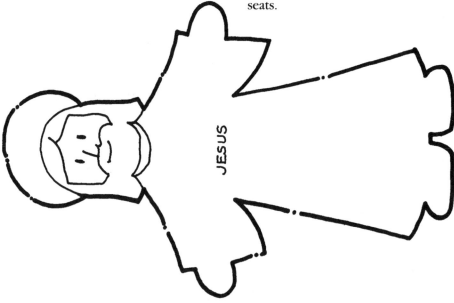

Matthew 18:15-20

"If your brother sins against you, go to him and show him his fault. Do it privately, just between yourselves. If he listens to you, you have won your brother back." (Matthew 18:15, *Today's English Version***)**

Summary

In this reading from the Gospel of Matthew, Jesus offers a loving method for dealing with conflict. In today's homily, children discuss how to handle a family conflict, then hear the story from today's gospel.

Materials

Bible

Homily

Invite the children to come forward for today's homily. Ask them to be seated in a semicircle around you.

Tell the children this unfinished story:

■ You like to watch cartoons on Saturday morning, but your older brother wants to watch reruns of a show that you don't like. One Saturday, you are up before anyone else. You begin watching cartoons. Right in the middle of one cartoon, your brother comes in and switches the channel.

Encourage the children to suggest their own endings for the story, including ideas about how to handle the conflict. You might ask:

■ What happens next?
■ How would you feel if that happened?
■ How would your older brother (or sister) feel?
■ How will you treat each other the next day? Why?
■ Jesus told a story about what to do when we're angry, and that's the story I want to tell you today.

Hold the Bible open to the Gospel of Matthew as you tell today's story:

One day Jesus was talking to his disciples, the friends who listened to him teach. One of

71

his friends asked, "Jesus, you tell us to love one another, but what do we do if we are angry?"

Jesus did not say, "Do not be angry."

Jesus did not say, "You cannot ever quarrel."

Instead, Jesus said, "If your friend does something that hurts you or makes you sad, talk to your friend all by yourself. Tell your friend what is wrong."

"But what if my friend won't listen to me?" asked the friend. "What do I do then?"

"Then," Jesus answered, "take someone else with you. Maybe your friend will listen to both of you together."

"But," the disciple said, "what if my friend still won't listen?"

Jesus said, "Then you need even more help. You can always ask for help if you are having trouble with your friends."

If you wish, discuss:
- Have you ever made up with someone who was angry at you? What did you do? What happened next?
- What advice would you give to another child who was having a quarrel? What advice did Jesus have?

Prayer
- Thank you, Jesus, for showing us how to love people, even when we're mad at them. *Amen.*

Thank the children for joining you and invite them to return to their seats.

Matthew 18:21-35

Then Peter came to Jesus and asked, "Lord, if my brother keeps on sinning against me, how many times do I have to forgive him? Seven times?" (Matthew 18:21, *Today's English Version*)

Summary

In this reading from the Gospel of Matthew, Jesus illustrates the need for forgiveness by telling the parable of the unforgiving servant. In today's homily, children use beans to illustrate the forgiveness Jesus requires in today's story.

Materials

Bible
1 lb. dried beans, divided into: one bag of 490 beans and another bag with the extra beans
3 bowls

Homily

Invite the children to come forward for today's homily. Ask them to be seated in a semicircle around you.

Ask one or two of the children to count out seven beans from the bag of extra beans. Put these beans in one bowl. Let the children observe how many beans are in the bowl.

Now invite children to count out seventy beans, asking each of seven children each to count out ten beans. Place these beans in a separate bowl. Let the children ob-

serve how many beans are in the bowl.

Say:
■ Now let me show you seventy *times seven* beans.

Bring out bag of 490 beans, counted before the homily. Explain:
■ These are even more than seventy beans.
■ You would need seven bowls of these *(touch the seventy beans)* to make these *(touch the 490)*.

Explain that you will use the beans to tell today's story.

Note: This story uses an audience-participation refrain. Invite children to shout the response "Not enough!" whenever you ask, "Is that enough?" Practice this response once or twice before beginning the homily.

Hold the Bible open to the Gospel of Matthew as you tell today's story.

Jesus and Peter were walking. Peter was thinking.

That brother of mine, Peter was thinking. I'm sick and tired of that brother of mine!

"How many times?" said Peter aloud.

"How many times what?" asked Jesus.

"I've forgiven my brother before," said Peter. "Is that enough?" (*Not enough!*)

"I've forgiven my brother seven times!" said Peter. "Is that enough?" (*Not enough!*)

"Peter," said Jesus, "let me tell you a story. Once there was a servant who wanted money. He borrowed money from his king. The king asked, 'Is that enough?'" (*Not enough!*)

"The servant borrowed so much money he owed millions of dollars—more than he could ever repay. The king was angry. 'I can throw you into jail,' he said, "until you have paid every last penny.'

"The servant fell to his knees. 'Have mercy on me,' he begged.

"The king felt sorry for the servant. 'I will have mercy,' he said. 'I won't throw you into prison. Indeed, I forgive every penny you owe.'

"The servant walked away. He saw another servant, one who had borrowed a few dollars from him. He grabbed the servant by his neck.

"'Pay up!' he ordered. 'Or else!'

"The second servant fell to his knees. 'Have mercy on me,' he begged.

"'No,' said the first servant. And he threw the second servant into jail.

"The king heard and was angry. He sent for the wicked servant. 'Didn't I forgive you?' the master asked. 'Shouldn't you have forgiven another?'

"And so, Peter, I ask you, if you forgive another person seven times (*touch the bowl of seven beans*), is that enough?" (*Not enough!*)

"If you forgive another person seventy times (*touch the bowl of seventy beans*), is that enough?" (*Not enough!*)

"I tell you, you must forgive one another seventy times seven. (*Pour the 490 beans, in a steady stream, from the bag into the third bowl.*) You must forgive one another without end."

If you wish, discuss:
- When is forgiving hard?
- What can we do to help us forgive others?

Prayer
- Thank you, Jesus, for telling us about forgiveness. Help us, God, to forgive and forgive and forgive…just like you. *Amen.*

Thank the children for joining you and invite them to return to their seats.

■　■　■　■　■

Matthew 20:1-16

"The Kingdom of heaven is like this. Once there was a man who went out early in the morning to hire some men to work in his vineyard." (Matthew 20:1, *Today's English Version*)

Summary

In this reading from the Gospel of Matthew, Jesus tells the story of the generous vineyard owner, illustrating God's generosity to all. In today's homily, children hear Jesus' parable, then identify many ways in which God is generous to them.

Materials

Bible
1 baskets, 1 empty, 1 filled with coins

Homily

Invite the children to come forward for today's homily. Ask them to be seated in a semicircle around you.

Hold the Bible open to the Gospel of Matthew as you tell today's story:

A man goes into his vineyard. The sun shines, making the vineyard bright and warm. Delicious, sweet grapes grow in the vineyard.

"My grapes are ready to pick," the man says. "I need help."

He goes to the first worker. "Will you help me pick my sweet grapes?" the man asks. "I will pay you a silver coin."

"Yes!" says the first worker. He goes to the vineyard and picks grapes. But there are so many grapes to pick!

"I need more help," said the man.

He goes to the second worker. "Will you help me pick my ripe grapes?" the man asks. "I will pay you, too."

"Yes!" says the second worker. He goes to the vineyard and picks grapes. But there are still so many grapes to pick.

"I want more help," says the man.

He goes to the third worker. "Will you help me pick my delicious grapes?" the man asks. "I will pay you, too."

"Yes!" says the third worker. He goes to the vineyard and picks grapes. Soon the workday is done.

"I picked ten baskets of grapes," says the first worker.

"I picked three baskets of grapes," says the second worker.

"I picked only one basket," says the third worker.

"I will pay you all," says the man. He gives the worker who picked only one basket one silver coin. He gives the worker who picked three baskets one silver coin. He gives the worker who picked ten baskets one silver coin.

"That's not fair!" says the first worker. "I was first. I picked the most. I want the most money."

But the man who owns the vineyard says,

"I love the last,
The middle, the first.
Each gets one coin,
From my purse.

"I want to give the last worker as much as the first worker," says the man. And so he does.

Place the two baskets (one empty, one filled with coins) in front of the children. Say:

■ The owner in today's story chose to be kind to all the workers. He gave each and every worker a silver coin. *(Drop a coin into the empty basket.)*

■ Jesus says God is like the owner because God is kind, too. God gives each of us good things.

■ What good things does God give us? *(Drop a coin for each good thing named into the empty basket. If necessary, name several good things yourself to start the responses flowing. Possible responses include our families, our friends, our church, etc.)*

Prayer

■ Dear God, thanks for giving us so many good things. Help us to these good gifts with others. *Amen.*

Thank the children for joining you and invite them to return to their seats.

■ ■ ■ ■ ■

Matthew 21:28-32

"Which one of the two did what the father wanted?" (Matthew 21:31, *Today's English Version*)

Summary

In this reading from the Gospel of Matthew, Jesus tells the parable of the two sons, who are asked by their father to help in the vineyard. Jesus uses the parable to illustrate the greater importance of our actions, not our words. In today's homily, children practice making choices, then hear today's gospel story about an important choice.

Materials

Bible
2 different toys
pictures of 2 different pets, for
    example, a cat and a dog, or a
    turtle and a parakeet
2 kinds of small treats for children,
    for example, pretzels and potato
    chips, or chocolate covered
    peanuts and jelly beans

Homily

Invite the children to come forward for today's homily. Ask them to be seated in a semicircle around you.

Lead the children in a discussion of choices. Hold up the two different toys and ask:
- If you could choose, which of these two toys would you rather play with? Hold up your hand nice and high if you'd rather

play with *(name toy)*. Hold up your hand nice and high if you'd rather play with *(name other toy)*.
- Sometimes having choices is fun, isn't it?

Hold up the pictures of two different pets. Ask:
- If you could choose, which of these two pets would you rather have at home? Who would rather have a *(name one of the pets)?* Who would rather have a *(name the other pet)?*
- Why does it feel good to be able to choose sometimes?

Offer children the option to help themselves to *one* each of *one* of the treats. Ask:
- Why did you choose the treat you chose?
- Do you like the choice you made?
- Jesus tells about important choices in today's story.

Hold the Bible open to the Gospel of Matthew as you tell today's story:

Once there was a father with two sons.

The father said to his older son, "The grapes are ripe. I want you to work in the vineyard today and pick those grapes."

The son thought, "I don't feel like working all day in the hot sun. I want to see my friends today." So he said to his father, "No. I don't want to go."

The father sighed and went to his second son. "The grapes are ripe," he said. "I want you to work in the vineyard today and pick those grapes."

This son said, very politely, "Yes, father, of course I will!"

But the first son had been thinking things over. "My father wants my help," he said to himself. "If I don't help, the grapes might spoil. I will do what my father wants."

And he went to the vineyard to work hard all day.

But the second son never left his room. He said to himself, "I don't really want to work today. I can always tell my father that I didn't feel well."

The second son never went to the vineyard at all.

Jesus asked, "Which son do you think did what his father wanted?"

Allow time for children to answer this final question.

Prayer

- Thank you, God, for giving us choices. Help us to make wise and loving choices. *Amen.*

Thank the children for joining you and invite them to return to their seats.

■ ■ ■ ■ ■

Matthew 21:33-43

"Listen to another parable," Jesus said. "There was once a landowner who planted a vineyard, put a fence around it, dug a hole for the wine press, and built a watchtower. Then he rented the vineyard to tenants and left home on a trip." (Matthew 21:33, *Today's English Version*)

Summary

In this reading from the Gospel of Matthew, Jesus tells the parable of the tenants in the vineyard. In today's homily, children explore the fruit of a vineyard, then hear today' story, seeing themselves under God's care as if they were a treasured vineyard.

Materials

Bible
grape juice
1 bunch of grapes
raisins
cups
napkins

Homily

Invite the children to come forward for today's homily. Ask them to be seated in a semicircle around you.

Hold up the bunch of grapes for children to see. Ask:
■ What are these?
■ That's right; they are grapes.

Grapes grow on vines in vineyards. Today's story is about a man who grows grapes in his vineyard.
■ Who here has eaten grapes?

Give a grape to each child who would like one. Hold up a raisin. Ask:
■ What is this?
■ That's right, a raisin. Did you know that every raisin used to be a grape? A raisin is a dried grape.

Give a raisin to each child who would like one. Hold up the grape juice. Ask:
■ Who can tell me what this is?
■ That's right, it's grape juice. It's juice that's made from grapes. People squeeze grapes and collect the juice so we can drink it.

Give each child a small cup of grape juice. Say:
■ Vineyards grow good things to eat.
■ Let's listen to today's story about a vineyard.

Hold the Bible open to the Gospel of Matthew as you tell today's story:

A man says, "I want to grow grapes in my vineyard. I want thick, healthy vines, big green leaves, and sweet ripe grapes."

The man helps the grapes grow. First the man digs into the dirt and picks out the stones.

Carefully he plants young grape plants.

He puts a fence all around his vineyard to keep out wild animals.

The man says, "I love the sweet, ripe grapes. I love my vineyard very much."

God says, "I want people. I want old people, boys and girls, babies, grownups, and teenagers. I want many, many people."

God helps the people grow. God gives food, air, and water to the people.

God gives families and friends to the people.

God even sends Jesus to help people grow happy and strong.

God says, "I love all the different people. (*If possible, name each child.*) I love my people very much."

Prayer

Discuss with the children:
- God takes care of the vineyard.
- God takes care of us, too.
- How does God take care of you?
- For what would you like to thank God today?

Allow children who wish to respond to do so. Close by praying:
- God, thank you for taking care of us. Help us to grow with you forever. *Amen.*

Thank the children for joining you and invite them to return to their seats.

■ ■ ■ ■ ■

Matthew 22:1-10

"The Kingdom of heaven is like this. Once there was a king who prepared a wedding feast for his son." (Matthew 22:2, *Today's English Version*)

Summary

In this reading from the Gospel of Matthew, Jesus tells a parable that compares the kingdom of God to a king's feast. In today's homily, children participate in the telling of the story.

Materials

Bible
tablecloth
plates, cups, napkins and silverware, enough for 2 place settings
candlesticks
platter with treats for children, for example, cookies, small candy bars, pretzels, etc.

Homily

Invite the children to come forward for today's homily. Ask them to be seated in a semicircle around you.

Begin the homily by spreading the tablecloth in the center of the circle of children. Set up the candlesticks, plates, napkins, cups and silverware picnic-style on the tablecloth. Add the plate of treats. As you spread this "feast," discuss with the children:

■ What do you think the word *feast* means? *(Accept the children's ideas. As necessary, add,*

"The way I will use the word in today's story is this: a feast is a big party with a special meal.")

■ What kinds of special meals do our families have for special days?

■ What favorite food do you like having at these special meals?

■ Let's listen to a story Jesus told about a special meal.

Hold the Bible open to the Gospel of Matthew as you tell today's story:

Knocking loudly at the door, a messenger boomed, "By royal proclamation, you are invited to a party at the palace. The king's son is getting married, and you are invited to the wedding feast."

The storekeeper stuck her head out the door. "We're not open yet," she said. "And besides, why should I go to a party at the palace? Not for me. Nope."

Another messenger was calling out to the farmer, working in the fields.

"By royal proclamation, you are invited to a party at the palace, " boomed the messenger across the field. "The king's son is..."

"Forget it," called the farmer. "It's time for me to get in my crops. I can't be going to any parties!"

House after house, field after field, the messengers found no one who would come to the king's feast. When at last they made their tired way back to the king, all they could say was, "We tried, O king, but no one you invited would come."

The king was furious. He said, "The people I invited did not deserve my invitation. They will not come to my feast. Instead, go out into the streets and invite new guests. Invite everyone you can find, and do not forget the blind, those who cannot walk, and those who are poor."

Back ran the messengers to the streets of the city. "By royal proclamation, you are invited to a party at the palace," called the messengers.

"Oh, yes!" said a blind person. "I will come."

"Thank you!" said a person who could not walk. "I will come."

"A *party*!" said a homeless person. "Oh, how I would love to come to the king's party."

"Will there be cookies? Will there be balloons?" asked the children. "Can we come, too?"

"Yes," said the messenger, "*All* are welcome at the king's feast."

Soon the wedding hall doors were opened. Soon the hall filled with people—making music, dancing and feasting.

"This is the most wonderful feast there ever was!" said the people. "Surely everyone wants to come to this feast!"

But when the king heard this, he gave a sad smile. "I wish everyone *would* come to my feast," he said.

Affirm for the children that everyone in church this morning—pastors, teachers, moms and dads, friends, *children—all* are welcome at God's feast. Invite each child to enjoy a cookie from the feast spread before them.

Prayer

■ Thank you, God, for asking each one of us to come to your special feast. *Amen.*

Thank the children for joining you and invite them to return to their seats.

■ ■ ■ ■ ■

Matthew 22:15-21

Jesus said to them, "Well, then, pay to the Emperor what belongs to the Emperor, and pay to God what belongs to God." (Matthew 22:21b, *Today's English Version*)

Summary

In this reading from the Gospel of Matthew, Jesus answers the Pharisees' question about paying taxes. In today's homily, children hear this story and discuss what it means to give to God.

Materials

Bibles
collection plate or basket used in your church
box containing:
    canned food item
    Bible
    article of clothing
    plastic adhesive bandage strip
    pair of shoes
    candle

Homily

Invite the children to come forward for today's homily. Ask them to be seated in a semicircle around you.

Hold the Bible open to the Gospel of Matthew as you tell today's story.

Once some people asked Jesus a question.

"What belongs to God?" they asked. "What belongs to us?"

Jesus said, "God makes everything. God makes cats and dogs, turtles and mice." Can you name other animals made by God? *(Invite children to name many kinds of animals.)* "All animals belong to God," said Jesus.

"God makes pine trees and palm trees, sunflowers and green grass." Can you name other growing things made by God? *(Invite children to name many kinds of plants and trees.)* "All plants belong to God," said Jesus.

"God makes moms and dads, grandmothers and grandfathers, aunts and uncles." Can you name other people made by God? *(Invite children to name many kinds of people. Children can also name specific people.)* "All people belong to God," said Jesus.

"God makes rivers and rocks, clouds and stars." Can you name other things made by God? *(Invite children to name other objects.)* "Everything in creation belongs to God," said Jesus.

83

"Then what belongs to us?"
the people asked.

"Everything on earth," said
Jesus. "God gives you every-
thing God makes."

"Can we give anything to God?"
asked the people.

"Yes," said Jesus. "You can give
God thanks and praise."

Show children the collection basket or plate used in church. Ask:
- What is this?
- When have we seen this collection basket used?
- What do people put into this
  basket?
- Bible people brought offering
  money to their temple just as
  we bring our offerings to
  church.
- Giving to our church is one way
  we can give to God.
- *(Direct children's attention to*
  the box of items.) In this box
  are some of the things that we
  buy with the money we give in
  church.
- Listen and guess what's in the
  box. Keep your guesses a secret
  until I'm done telling you each
  clue.

Read each clue printed below and
let the children guess what item
you are describing. Then remove
that item from the box and show it
to the children. *Clues:*
- People in church give money to
  buy boxes and cans of me. I
  show love when the church
  gives me away. People who are
  hungry need me very much.
  (can of food)
- I am the special book of the

Church. You hear my words
every time you come to church.
Children hear my words in
church and at home. Even very
old people love my words,
because you are never too old
for me! *(Bible)*
- I come in all sizes and shapes.
  I keep people warm when it's
  cold. People in church buy different kinds of me for people
  who need me. *(clothing)*
- I am little, but very important.
  The money from our church
  buys me and lots of other things
  like me for people who are sick.
  When you get a cut, you need
  me. *(adhesive bandage strip)*
- You need me when you go outside, but some people can't buy
  me. The church buys me in lots
  of different sizes for others who
  don't have a pair of me. I keep
  your feet warm and dry. *(shoes)*
- I am tall and beautiful. You see
  me at the front of the church on
  a special table. I am used up as I
  make a lovely, tiny flame of fire.
  (candle)

When you have finished all clues
and guesses, invite children to share
what they hope their offering
money buys. Remind children
that God loves to receive their gifts,
and each gift helps people who
re hungry, sick, lonely or wanting
toknow God.

Prayer

- God, thanks you for sharing
  your big, wonderful world with
  us. *Amen.*

Thank the children for joining you
and invite them to return to their
seats.

■ ■ ■ ■ ■

Matthew 22:34-40

Jesus answered, "'Love the Lord your God with all your heart, with all your soul, and with all your mind.'" (Matthew 22:37, *Today's English Version*)

Summary

In this reading from the Gospel of Matthew, Jesus summarizes all of scripture with one command: *Love!* In today's homily, children first hear the gospel story, then suggest and practice ways to love God and others.

Materials

Bible

Homily

Invite the children to come forward for today's homily. Ask them to be seated in a semicircle around you.

Hold the Bible open to the Gospel of Matthew as you tell today's story.

In Bible times people often argued, just as we do today. Jesus' disciples sometimes argued about which one Jesus loved best. Teachers of God's laws sometimes argued about what scripture really meant.

One of these teachers said to Jesus, "Jesus, there are many laws of God in the Bible. Which law do you think is most important?"

Jesus said, "The most important law is to love God, with your whole heart and your whole soul and your whole strength. The next most important law is to love other people just as much as you do yourself."

"Is that what you want us to do?" asked another person.

"Yes," said Jesus. "I want you to love God. I want you to love others. I want you to love yourselves. Those are the best things to do!"

Discuss with the children:
■ What rules did Jesus say were most important? *(love God; love others and ourselves)*
■ How do we show God that we love God?

Welcome and affirm all responses from the children. When a child suggests a way to love God that could be immediately demonstrated, do so. *Examples:*

- If children say, "Pray to God," then say, "Let's do that now" and offer a short, simple prayer; for example, "God, we show we love you by praying to you. *Amen.*"
- If children say, "Sing in church," then sing a familiar chorus with them, inviting the parishioners to join in.

After several ways to love God have been suggested and demonstrated, ask:

- And how can we show that we love others?

Again, welcome and affirm children's answers, putting into immediate practice as many suggestions as possible. *Examples*:

- Exchange hugs.
- Say, "I love you."
- Share a piece of candy.

Be sure to involve the parishioners. Children will more deeply appreciate their importance in the life of the church when they see their suggestions implemented by a church full of people.

Prayer

- Loving God, you call us to love you and each other and ourselves. Help us to discover more and more fun ways to do love. *Amen.*

Thank the children for joining you and invite them to return to their seats.

■ ■ ■ ■ ■

Matthew 23:1-12

"Whoever makes himself great will be humbled, and whoever humbles himself will be made great." (Matthew 23:12, *Today's English Version*)

Summary

In this reading from the Gospel of Matthew, Jesus teaches that honor and prestige are not nearly as important to God as acts of service to others. In today's homily, children hear today's story, then talk about ways in which they serve others.

Materials

Bible
"The Greatest" badges (see **note** below)

Note: Before the homily create several "The Greatest" badges, 1 per every 3-4 children you expect to come forward for the homily. Copy the illustration below as you follow these steps:
■ Cut circles from construction paper, about 3" in diameter. Use felt markers to write *The Greatest* on each circle.
■ Cut star-like backgrounds from a contrasting color of construction paper to place behind the first circle.
■ Use wide wrapping-paper or cloth ribbon to hang from the back of each badge.
■ Glue or tape the badges together.
■ Affix a circle of masking tape to the back of each badge so that

the badges will stick to children's clothing.

(If you typically have only a few children come forward for the homily, make one badge per child and plan to let each child keep a badge at the conclusion of the homily.)

Homily

Invite the children to come forward for today's homily. Ask them to be seated in a semicircle around you.

Invite one of the children to read aloud the words written on one of the badges. Ask:
■ If you could give this badge to anyone in the whole world, to whom would you give it? Why?

Encourage many responses. Be sure to repeat quieter answers so the parishioners can hear them as well. Conclude by saying:

- Once Jesus talked about important people, too, and that's the story I want to tell you today.

Hold the Bible open to the Gospel of Matthew as you tell today's story:

Jesus' friends had arguments, just like any friends. One argument they had over and over was, "Who is really important?"

One friend said, "Maybe kings are the most important people. They sit on thrones and tell everyone what to do."

Another friend said, "Maybe rich people are the most important. They can buy anything they want."

But one friend said, "Maybe religion teachers are the most important. They tell us what God wants us to do."

Now all the friends said, "Yes, they must be the most important people of all. Look how people give them the best seats and do whatever the teachers tell them."

But Jesus said, "Look at what a person does, not what a person says.

"If religion teachers think they should get the best seats, I do not think they are the most important people.

"If religion teachers make you do hard things, but do not do hard things themselves, I do not think they are the most important people.

"If religion teachers are bossy and mean, I do not think they are the most important people," said Jesus. "I do not want my friends to be like that."

"Well, who *is* important," asked one friend.

"You are all brothers and sisters," said Jesus. "You are all important to me. And I think the most important people are those who help others."

Ask:
- Who does Jesus think are the most important people? *(those who help others)*
- What are some of the ways we've helped others this last week?

As each child suggests a way in which he or she helped another, help stick one of "The Greatest" badges on the child. When all the badges have been placed on children, ask the children wearing the badges to transfer them to other children as each new child suggests a way he or she has helped others.

When all children who wish to share a way in which they have helped others have done so, and even those who haven't shared but would like to wear the badge have also done so, collect the badges.

Prayer
- Thank you, God, for giving us so many people to love us and help us. Help us to help others, too. *Amen.*

Thank the children for joining you and invite them to return to their seats.

Matthew 24:42-44

"So then, you also must always be ready, because the Son of Man will come at an hour when you are not expecting him." (Matthew 24:44, *Today's English Version***)**

Summary

In this reading from the Gospel of Matthew, Jesus urges us always to be ready, for his eventual return will come without announcement. In today's homily, children talk about "getting ready," then listen and respond to today's gospel story.

Materials

Bible

Homily

Invite the children to come forward for today's homily. Ask them to be seated in a semicircle around you.

Say to the children:
- Let's imagine we are getting ready to go camping. What are some of the things we want to take?
- Imagine we are camping, and dinnertime comes. We're hungry! What do we need? Did anyone bring what we need? *(food, cooking equipment, etc.)*
- Imagine it is late at night and we are sleepy. What do we need? Did anyone bring what we need? *(pillows, sleeping bags, etc.)*
- In the middle of the night, we

hear an interesting sound. Maybe it's a bird or an animal we would like to see. What do we need to help us see at night? Did anyone bring what we need? *(flashlight, lantern, matches, etc.)*

Continue:
- Planning what to bring is one way we get ready to go camping.
- How do we get ready for a birthday party? for school? to play a game?
- We get ready in many different ways, for many special times.
- In today's story, Jesus also tells about being ready. Let's listen.

Hold the Bible open to the Gospel of Matthew as you tell today's story:

One day Jesus' friends asked him, "When will you come again? How will people know you are coming?"

"I am coming again," said Jesus. "But even I don't know when I will come. Only God knows.

"So wait for me," said Jesus. "Watch for me. I will surprise everyone when I come.

"I am coming to bring light wherever it's dark. I am coming to bring peace wherever there's hurt. I am coming to bring good news to God's people.

"Wait for me! Watch for me!"

Discuss with the children:
■ In today's gospel, Jesus tells us we should always be ready for the day when Jesus comes again.
■ How could we get ready for Jesus' coming? (*Encourage chil dren to give as many answers as possible.*)

If children need extra help in answering this question, say:
■ One way to get ready for Jesus is to show love for God. How can we show love for God?
■ Another way to get ready for Jesus is to show love for other people. How can we show love for other people?

Prayer

■ Jesus, we look forward to your coming. Help us to welcome you, every day. *Amen.*

Thank the children for joining you and invite them to return to their seats.

■ ■ ■ ■ ■

Matthew 25:1-13

And Jesus concluded, "Watch out, then, because you do not know the day or the hour." (Matthew 25:13, *Today's English Version*)

Summary

In this reading from the Gospel of Matthew, Jesus tells the parable of the ten girls and their oil lamps, illustrating the need to be ready for his second coming. In today's homily, the children hear today's story, then talk briefly about wise and foolish choices *or* sing "This Little Light of Mine."

Materials

Bible
discarded pair of light-colored gloves (yellow rubber kitchen gloves or cloth gardening gloves work well)
fine-point felt marker
optional:
colored felt markers

Note: Before the homily, use the fine-point marker to draw ten faces, one on each fingertip of the gloves. (In a pinch, you could also draw the faces directly on your fingertips using washable markers.) If you wish, add other features using colored markers, like hair, clothes, etc. You will use the gloves (or your fingertips) as puppets as you tell today's story.

Homily

Invite the children to come forward for today's homily. Ask them to be seated in a semicircle around you.

Before putting on the gloves and telling today's story, discuss:
■ Who knows what the word *wise* means?

Welcome and affirm all answers. If necessary, define *wise* as *making good choices*. Continue:
■ Who knows what the word *foolish* means?

Again affirm all answers. If necessary, define *foolish* as *making bad choices*. Put on the gloves and say:
■ Here is a story that Jesus told about five wise girls *(wiggle one set of fingers)* and five foolish girls *(wiggle the other set of fingers)*.

Place the Bible nearby—open to the Gospel of Matthew—as you tell today's story:

Once there were ten girls who were waiting to go to a wonderful party. *(Wiggle all the fingers.)* They were waiting to hear the words, "Come to the party!" Then it would be time to go.

The ten girls waited. *(Wiggle fingers.)* And waited. *(Wiggle, a little less enthusiastically.)* And waited. *(Barely move the fingers at all.)*

By now it was dark outside, almost time for bed. One by one the girls fell asleep. *(Let the fingers collapse, one at a time.)*

Suddenly they heard a shout. "It's almost time for the party! Be sure you bring your lamp!" The girls woke in a hurry! *(Let the ten fingers spring up.)*

The five foolish girls looked at their lamps. *(Bend fingers of one hand toward central point.)* The lamps were almost empty of oil. "Oh, no," the foolish girls cried. "Our lamps are almost ready to go out!" And they ran off into the night to look for oil for their lamps. *(Make these fingers scurry away.)*

Now came the voice the girls had been waiting for. "It's time! Come to the party!" And the five wise girls picked up their lamps and went off to the wonderful party. *(Let these five fingers dance away.)*

But the five foolish girls never went to the party at all.

After the story, discuss with the children:
- Who made wise choices in today's story?
- Who made foolish choices in today's story?
- When can we make wise choices each day?

or

Lead children in singing "This Little Light of Mine." You could add these motions:

> This little light of mine,
>   *(Cup hands.)*
> I'm gonna let it shine.
>   *(Raise arms up and out.)*
> This little light of mine,
>   *(Cup hands.)*
> I'm gonna let it shine.
>   *(Raise arms up and out.)*
> Let it shine. Let it shine. Let it shine.
>   *(Raise arms up and wave as you turn in a circle.)*

Prayer

- Help us, Jesus, to be ready to shine as lights for you. *Amen.*

Thank the children for joining you and invite them to return to their seats.

Matthew 25:14-20

"'Well done, you good and faithful servant!' said his master. 'You have been faithful in managing small amounts, so I will put you in charge of large amounts. Come on in and share my happiness!'" (Matthew 25:21, *Today's English Version*)

Summary

In this reading from the Gospel of Matthew, Jesus tells the parable of the three servants, whose master expects them to use the gifts they have been given. In today's homily, the children experiment with many different gifts God has given them, then hear a version of today's gospel story.

Materials

Bible
10 pennies

Homily

Invite the children to come forward for today's homily. Ask them to *stand* in a semicircle around you.

Begin the homily by inviting children to share things that they can do with their legs and feet, for example, run, hop, gallop, jump, etc. When appropriate, invite children to briefly demonstrate each of these as they are suggested.

Continue by inviting children to share things they can do with their arms and hands, for example, wave, shake hands, clap, make a sandwich, etc. Again, ask children to demonstrate those actions when appropriate.

Finally, invite children to share things they can do with their mouths, for example, sing, shout, talk, smack lips, etc. These, too, can be demonstrated, as appropriate.

Say:
- God gives us bodies—legs, feet, arms, hands and mouths.
- When we run fast, we use the legs God gives us.
- When we sing, we use the mouth God gives us.
- What do you like to do best?
- How do you use what God gives you?
- Jesus told a story about using what God has given us, and that's the story I want to tell you today.

Ask the children to be seated. Hold the Bible open to the Gospel of Matthew as you tell today's story:

Once there were two men. One man said to the other, "Here. I give you five pennies." *(Set out a pile of five pennies.)*

This man used the five pennies to earn five more. *(Add a second set of five to the first set.)*

"Here," he said. "Here are the five pennies you gave me and five more than I earned."

"Good job!" the first man said. "I am happy to see how you used my gift."

Here is a woman and a child. God says, "Woman, I give you the gift of telling stories."

God says, "Child, I give you the gift of running and jumping."

All day long the child runs and jumps. "I love to run and jump," says the child.

That night, at bedtime, the woman tells the child a story. "Thank you for the story," says the child.

"I love to tell you stories," says the woman.

"Good job!" says God. "I am happy to see you run, child. I am happy to hear your stories, woman. I am happy to see how you use my gifts."

Prayer

- Thank you, God, for all you give us. Thank you for all we can do. *Amen.*

Thank the children for joining you and invite them to return to their seats.

■ ■ ■ ■ ■

Matthew 25:31-46

"The King will reply, 'I tell you, whenever you did this for one of the least important of these followers of mine, you did it for me'" (Matthew 25:40, *Today's English Version*)

Summary

In this reading from the Gospel of Matthew, Jesus explains that we are serving him whenever we serve someone in need. In today's homily, the children hear today's gospel story, then pantomime the acts of compassion described in today's gospel.

Materials

Bible
several plates and bowls
several cups
several sweaters or jackets

Homily

Invite the children to come forward for today's homily. Ask them to be seated in a semicircle around you.

Hold the Bible open to the Gospel of Matthew as you tell today's story:

Some day Jesus will come again as King. All the people in the world will be before him. Then he will call certain people.

He will say to them, "Come on in! Come into God's kingdom, because I was hungry and you fed me."

He will say, "Come on in! Come into God's kingdom, because I was thirsty and you gave me something to drink."

He will say, "Come on in! Come into God's kingdom, because I was cold and you gave me clothes to wear."

He will say, "Come on in! Come into God's kingdom, because I was sad and lonely and you came to me."

Then these people will say, "When did we do that? When did we ever see you hungry and feed you?

They will say, "When did we do that? When did we ever see you thirsty and give you something to drink?"

95

They will say, "When did we do that? When did we ever see you cold and give you clothes to wear?"

They will say, "When did we do that? When did we ever see you lonely and come to you?"

And King Jesus will answer, "I saw you do these things for other people—for children, grownups and strangers. Whenever you did this for someone else, you did it for me, too!"

Invite children to pantomime the acts of compassion described in today's gospel. Introduce the activity by discussing:

■ What did the friends of Jesus do in today's gospel reading? How did they help others?

Ask children to pantomime the following situations. As one situation gets underway, start children on another. All situations can be pantomimed simultaneously, and children can feel free to leave one situation and join another. Use as many situations as time and space allow:

■ Ask several children to pretend to be very hungry. Set other children to work chopping make-believe vegetables for a soup, stirring and pouring imaginary soup into imaginary cups for the hungry ones, etc.

■ Ask children to pretend to be thirsty. Let volunteers pour make-believe glasses of water and distribute them to those who are thirsty.

■ Ask children to pretend to be lonesome and looking for friends. Other children can pantomime reading a story or playing a game together.

■ Ask children to shiver and shake from pretend cold. Let other children bundle them in sweaters or jackets and invite them to sit inside by a warm fireplace.

After a minute or two of pantomiming, discuss:

■ How do you feel when you help someone?

■ How does it feel to be helped?

Prayer

■ Jesus, you ask us to help those who are hurting and lonely. We want to do that for you. *Amen.*

Thank the children for joining you and invite them to return to their seats.

■ ■ ■ ■ ■

Matthew (21:1-10)
26:26–28:7

"He is not here; he has been raised, just as he said. Come here and see the place where he was lying." (Matthew 28:6, *Today's English Version*)

Summary

This reading from the Gospel of Matthew spans a large section of scripture, from Jesus' entry into Jerusalem, through his crucifixion, entombment and resurrection. Why include the resurrection? Because children always need to hear the story of Jesus' death completed by the story of his resurrection.

In today's homily, children participate in a condensed version of this story. If you don't wish to include the entry into Jerusalem as part of today's story, omit Center One and begin the story at the asterisk.

Materials

Note: Before the homily, arrange the materials listed below in four separate areas at the front of the church. During the homily, you will walk with children from Center One to Center Two to Center Three to Center Four.

For Center One:
palm branches, 1 per child (if necessary, substitute any branches)

For Center Two:
plate
cup
bread

For Center Three:
cross
block of scrap wood
hammer
large nail

For Center Four:
table or chair
sheet, blanket or tablecloth
pillow or cushion

Note: At Center Four, drape the sheet or blanket over three sides of the table or chair to make a tomb. Use the pillow or cushion as the rock that blocks the entrance to the tomb.

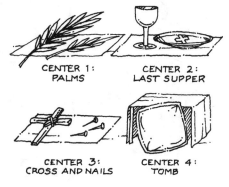

CENTER 1: PALMS   CENTER 2: LAST SUPPER

CENTER 3: CROSS AND NAILS   CENTER 4: TOMB

Homily

Invite the children to come forward for today's homily. Gather at Center One.

Carry the Bible with you—open to the Gospel of Matthew—as you tell today's story:

Jesus came to the holy city, Jerusalem. People were so excited to see Jesus that they picked branches from the trees and waved them. *(Pick up a palm branch. Wave it and call out, "Hosanna, Jesus! Save us now, Jesus!" Encourage the children to join you. Then lay down the branches and walk to Center Two—the Last Supper.)*

*Jesus ate one last time with all his friends. He took bread and prayed, "Thank you, God, for bread." He broke the bread. He gave the bread to his friends. "Do this to remember me," Jesus said.** *(Use the plate and bread to perform these actions; pick up the plate, lift it high as you give thanks and pass it around to all the children.)* **He took a cup of wine and prayed, "Thank you, God, for wine." He drank the wine. He shared the wine with his friends. "Do this to remember me," Jesus said.** *(Use the empty cup to perform these actions.)*

Jesus said, "I am so sad, my friends, because now I must leave you. *(Encourage children to exchange hugs with one an*

98

other.) **The time has come for me to die—but remember, God will give me new life."**

Soldiers came. They took Jesus away from his friends. *(Slowly walk to Center Three.)* **Jesus was sad and afraid.**

The soldiers made Jesus carry a cross. *(Pick up the cross; pass it from child to child.)* **Jesus stretched out his arms on the cross.** *(Stretch out your arms in a cross shape; encourage the children to join you.)* **Soldiers hammered nails in Jesus' hands and feet on the cross.** *(Hammer the nail into the wood several times. Do not invite the children to join in at this time.)*

Then Jesus hung on the cross until he died. *(Stand in silence with the children for a few moments.)* **The friends of Jesus came. They took Jesus down from the cross. They carried his body to a tomb.** *(Slowly walk to Center Four.)*

Jesus' friends put Jesus in the tomb. *(Mime this action.)* **Soldiers rolled a large stone in front of the door, so that no one could get in.** *(Put the cushion in front of the open side.)*

Three days passed; then something amazing happened. *(Slowly move the cushion.)* **Early that morning the stone rolled away. Jesus came out of the tomb. Jesus was alive! Jesus would never die again!**

Prayer

Invite the children to hold hands as you pray:

■ Thank you, God, for giving life to Jesus. Thank you, God for giving life to these your children: *(name each child, if possible). Amen.*

Thank the children for joining you and invite them to return to their seats.

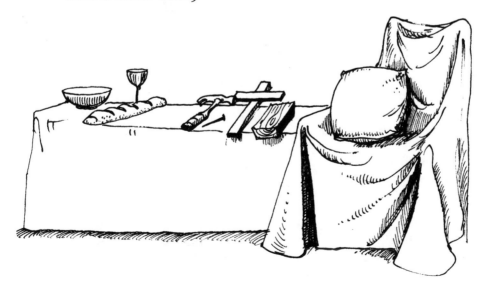

99

■ ■ ■ ■ ■

Matthew 28:1-10

"Do not be afraid," Jesus said to them. "Go and tell my brothers to go to Galilee, and there they will see me." (Matthew 28:10 *Today's English Version***)**

Summary

In this reading from the Gospel of Matthew, an angel announces to the women that Jesus is alive, the women meet Jesus as they return to Galilee, and Jesus pronounces a blessing of peace. In today's homily, children hear the story of Jesus' resurrection, share their feelings about this joyous event and create butterflies as reminders of resurrection life.

Materials

Bible
paper coffee filters, 1 per child
colored felt markers
pipe cleaners, 1 per child

Homily

Invite the children to come forward for today's homily. Ask them to be seated in a semicircle around you.

Hold the Bible open to the Gospel of Matthew as you tell today's story:

It was early in the morning, so early that the sky was just beginning to turn pink. Too early for birds to be singing.

Too early for people to be out walking.

But two people *were* **out walking. Two women. Two friends of Jesus. But they were feeling very sad. Jesus was dead. Jesus was buried in a cold, stone tomb. The women were on their way to look at the tomb, to cry by the tomb.**

Suddenly the ground began to rumble and shake! The women felt afraid. "What is happening?" they cried in alarm, holding each other. The shaking stopped, and they ran on to the tomb.

There they saw an amazing sight. An angel — bright like lightening, white like snow — sat on the big stone that blocked the entrance to the tomb. But the stone had been

moved! The tomb was open! The women looked at the angel. They looked at each other. They were too amazed to say a single word.

"Don't be afraid," said the angel. "You are looking for Jesus, but I have great news for you. Jesus is alive! Look, the tomb is empty! Go, tell your friends: Jesus is alive!"

The women hurried away, not knowing whether to feel frightened or joyful!

Then Jesus himself stood before them. "Peace be with you," he said.

The women fell to the ground before him. Jesus kept talking, "Don't be afraid. It's all true. I am alive. Go and tell our friends. Tell them I will see them soon."

And then the women knew they did not need to feel afraid anymore. Joy filled them. So much joy. So much happiness.

Invite children to respond:
- What did *you* hear in the story?
- What did you *imagine* as I told the story?

Invite children to make paper butterflies as symbols of resurrection life. Give each child a paper coffee filter. Invite the children to draw a few simple designs on the filter with colored markers. Gather each filter in the center and twist a pipe cleaner around it to secure the wings and make feelers.

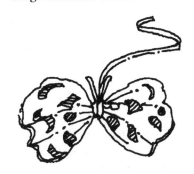

As children work, invite them to continue sharing their thoughts and feelings about Easter. Remember, when necessary, to repeat what children say for the benefit of the parishioners.

Invite the children to take their butterflies with them as reminders of Jesus' new, resurrection life.

Prayer
- Jesus, we are so glad you are alive. Thanks for sharing your resurrection life with each of us. *Amen.*

Thank the children for joining you and invite them to return to their seats.

Matthew 28:16-20

"Go, then, to all peoples everywhere and make them my disciples: baptize them in the name of the Father, the Son, and the Holy Spirit..." (Matthew 28:19, *Today's English Version*)

Summary

In this reading from the Gospel of Matthew, Jesus says farewell to disciples, commissioning them to take the good news of God's love to all the world and promising them that he will always be with them. In today's homily, children first hear the story, then decide on ways to take the news of God's love to others.

Materials

Bible
red or pink construction-paper hearts, several per child *(use the pattern printed below)*

Homily

Invite the children to come forward for today's homily. Ask them to be seated in a semicircle around you.

Hold the Bible open to the Gospel of Matthew as you tell today's story:

Jesus was alive again! He had been killed, but God raised him to new life. Jesus spent time with his friends. He ate with them, laughed with them and hugged them.

But now the time had come for him to leave. He said to his friends, "I have a special job for you:

"Go and tell people about me, people close to you and people far away. Tell them what I said. Tell them what I did.

"Tell them that God loves them."

Jesus' friends looked at each other. Tell everyone about Jesus? That would be a big job!

Jesus said, "It is a big job, but I have a promise for you too: You may not be able to see me or touch me, but always and forever, I will be with you."

Discuss with the children:

- What does Jesus want us to tell other people? *(tell them about Jesus; tell them that God loves them)*
- Let's start right now. Let's tell each other that God loves us.

Turn to a child next to you and say:
- God loves you, *(name of child).*

Ask that child to pass this blessing to the next child seated in the circle. Continue this blessing around the circle, assisting children as necessary.

Show the children one of the construction-paper hearts. Say:
- A heart like this is a symbol of love.
- I look at this heart, and I remember that God loves me.
- I look at this heart, and I remember that God loves *each of you.*

- I look at this heart, and I remember that Jesus asks me to tell others that God loves them, too.

Hand each child several of the construction-paper hearts. Say:
- After we pray, take your hearts with you as you return to your seats.
- You may keep one heart, but give your other hearts away to people you pass as you walk back or to the people seated around you.
- As you give away each heart, you might say, "God loves you!"

Prayer

- Jesus, thanks for asking us to let others know that God loves them. *Amen.*

Thank the children for joining you and invite them to return to their seats, passing out their extra hearts as they go.

103